BLUE COLLAR B & B
Adventures in Hospitality

BLUE COLLAR B & B
Adventures in Hospitality

*Dear Charlene —
Enjoy!
Bobby*

Bobby Hutchinson

LANGDON STREET PRESS
MINNEAPOLIS, MN

Copyright © 2009 by Bobby Hutchinson. All rights reserved.

Langdon Street Press
212 3rd Avenue North, Suite 290
Minneapolis, MN 55401
612.455.2293
www.langdonstreetpress.com

All rights reserved. No part of this publication may be reproduced, stored in a retrieval system, or transmitted, in any form or by any means, electronic, mechanical, photocopying, recording, or otherwise, without the written prior permission of the author.

ISBN - 978-1-934938-69-0
ISBN - 1-934938-69-6
LCCN - 2009930562

Book sales for North America and international:
Itasca Books, 3501 Highway 100 South, Suite 220
Minneapolis, MN 55416
Phone: 952.345.4488 (toll free 1.800.901.3480)
Fax: 952.920.0541; email to orders@itascabooks.com

Typeset by Peggy LeTrent

Printed in the United States of America

DEDICATED, WITH LOVE AND LAUGHTER, TO ALL MY GUESTS, PAST, PRESENT AND FUTURE—STAY LONG, TALK MUCH.

SO MUCH GRATITUDE:

TO—ALETHEA SPIRIDON, MY WONDERFUL EDITOR, FOR READING BLUE COLLAR SIX TIMES, DOING A SUPERB EDIT, AND THEN TELLING ME SHE STILL LOVED IT,

TO—ERIC, BRILLIANT PHOTOGRAPHER, TREASURED FRIEND, FOR MAKING ME LOOK BETTER ON THE BACK THAN I DO ON THE FRONT,

AND TO—NEAL EVAN CAMINSKY AND RED DREAM STUDIOS, FOR MY CANADIAN GOTHIC COVER.

Divorce is the mother of invention. Of course, necessity comes into it, but for me, divorce came first, which is why I decided, out of the fullness of my ignorance, to start a Bed and Breakfast. I needed money, and how hard could it be? I'd raised three strapping sons, I knew how to scrub bathrooms, change sheets, and make breakfasts Paul Bunyan would appreciate.

I was sixty-one, twice divorced, loved people but hated leaving my home to be among them. I'd been single two years. My house in Vancouver had a respectable west side address, a terrifying mortgage due to buying out my ex, and three empty bedrooms upstairs. My education consisted of a high school diploma from Sparwood High, located in a coal mining town in interior British Columbia, Canada. I'd married at eighteen, had a son at nineteen, and read my way through two more pregnancies (and several libraries) while trying to maintain sanity as I raised three diabolically inventive sons whose sole mission in life seemed either to commit suicide on my watch or live past adolescence—in jail.

My only saleable talent was writing steamy romance novels. I was far too old for prostitution, the only other job I could think of which might net enough to pay the mortgage. Writing earned me a fair living, but it was unpredictable. The urban myth about romance writers making mega bucks applies to those few exalted souls who make the coveted bestseller lists. There are others who turn out ten saleable properties a year, eating candy from a desk drawer, and sacrificing their health for thirty *good* pages a day. Their rule is: if you can't write better, write faster.

Of course, there are a few amazingly gifted people—Nora Roberts comes to mind—who can write both fast and really well. It's rumoured Nora will turn out an entire page turner while waiting in line for takeout Chinese.

Most of us are somewhere in between—nail-biting, coffee-guzzling peons who glue our respective asses to the chair each morning and churn out five pages a day, probably earning less in a year than the checkout girl at the local grocery store. Then why, people might ask, do we do it? We do it because we have to. Writing for us is like breathing—do it or die. I'd done it successfully forty-three times and despite the impressive number of published books gracing my mantle, I am far from wealthy, albeit grateful to Harlequin for my not-so-steady income.

Writing fiction is hit and miss—one's best, most brilliant ideas are often not what editors think will sell. Advance payments are always late. Most professional writers can finish a novel in the time it takes their publisher to send out the cheque originally meant to tide the starving writer through the creative process. If we're lucky, twice yearly royalties may pay the house taxes and the lawyer's fees with enough left over to go to Puerto Vallarta to recuperate from divorce and deadlines. Or, more probably, the cheque will barely buy a tank of gas. There's no surety in this writing game—you're only as good as your next novel, and you have to sell the damned proposal for that masterpiece before you can even write it.

Faced with shrinking markets and diminishing returns, I put a couple of notices on the Internet. I started with craigslist and added B&B International—might as well go from the ridiculous to the sublime. This is what I posted:

> *Blue Collar B&B.*
>
> *Stay in the heart of beautiful Vancouver with a romance writer who wants to hear your story. Reasonable rates, full breakfast. Close to golf links, shopping, and India town.*

JP Kinsella once said, *Build it and they will come.* Guess what? He was right.

THE JUNKMAN

"I polished up the handles so carefully,
They made me the ruler of the Queen's Navy."
—(Gilbert and Sullivan, HMS Pinafore)

Utterly petrified, I cowered in the kitchen as the doorbell announced my first guest. I'd checked the upstairs bathroom (pristine), the sheets on the king bed (freshly laundered, soft beige flannel, loosely tucked) and my hair and makeup, but at a certain age, there's only so much one can hope for in that department. Besides, he wasn't coming to date me, was he? He was coming to golf, his pert-sounding secretary had said. And he preferred B&B's to hotel rooms. Yippee for me. I was on my way to earning that few hundred extra a week I thought the B&B might bring, if I could only dredge up enough courage to answer the door.

It had dawned on me that not only had I never stayed at a B&B, I also didn't have the slightest clue how to run one. My one piece of advice, from my friend Patricia, who'd once operated a B&B with two toddlers underfoot while heavily pregnant with a third, was in answer to my query about sheets. How often should I change them if people stayed a week or longer? Pat thought it over. "Well, I think I'd definitely change them between guests," she advised.

So, I was on my own, and I didn't know how to do this. But I hadn't known how to write when I started, either. My rule of thumb has always been, the more you do a thing the better you get at it. In my case, it always worked, with the exception of marriage, of course.

The bell chimed again. A good beginning would probably be to open the front door. I took a deep calming breath, sucked in my belly, and there he was, smiling at me, my virgin bed and breakfaster.

"Hi, Bobby. I'm John Quinlan."

He was tall, handsome, fit looking —a good candidate for a hero in one of my books. Dark hair, good teeth, interesting eyebrows, squeaky clean. Forty-five, maybe. He heaved a small duffel and a large golf bag into my living room and set them on the rug, taking in the wall of bookshelves, the framed Klimt print of The Kiss, and the overstuffed furniture I'd inherited when my mother died. I'd tried to make up for its sagging cushions and bland tan colour by sewing a dozen silk pillows in a rainbow of bright colours and tossing them blithely around.

"Welcome, John. Did you have a good journey?" Too late, I remembered that he'd only come across from Vancouver Island, a mere two-and-a-half- hour ferry ride and forty minute drive.

"I did."

He had a great smile.

"It's always a good day when it isn't raining on the Lower Mainland. Nice place you have here. You do the landscaping yourself?"

"I have a gardener." I couldn't afford Mavis, but I couldn't fire her. She was forty-two and newly pregnant with her first baby by way of a much older man who wasn't yet divorced from his even older wife. Mavis was brilliant at unconventional landscaping. She'd turned my ordinary Vancouver lot into a showplace that had my oriental neighbours begging to see the back garden.

"I like the driftwood."

"Thanks. I always wanted a beach house, so we dragged that stuff home and covered all the grass with black plastic and then sand. Grass isn't my thing. What do people ever use it for?" Besides golf, I remembered too late. Oh God, what if he worshipped the stuff?

"I know what you mean. Grass needs way too much maintenance for what you get out of it."

Hey, I liked this guy. "Let me take your duffel. Your room is up these stairs." I led the way through the kitchen and made a sharp left, trying not to bang the bag, which was surprisingly heavy, against my newly washed walls, and also trying not to look as if I was about to have the Big One as I hoisted the bag up the stairs. At the top, I abandoned the cursed thing on the carpet in his room and tried to get my breath back without puffing audibly or giving in to the urge to collapse in a chair.

His eyes took in the gabled walls and the king sized bed wedged into an alcove. A wealthy, compassionate friend had given me the bed when I decided on the B&B knowing that the room had no furniture except for my desk and computer—which I'd now relocated.

The cartage men had warned me that if I ever moved, the bed stayed with the house. It had taken two husky specimens, cursing and sweating, to force the pillow top mattress up the narrow staircase and around the corner.

"Cozy," my guest declared, walking over to the window. "Is that a tree house down there?"

"It is." My friend Eric had built a narrow bridge from my back deck to the stately old cherry tree, and then designed and constructed an irregularly shaped tree house among the spreading branches. The result was kooky and vaguely Oriental, but then so was Eric.

"Feel free to use the hammock." We'd suspended a Himalayan sitting hammock, orange and green and gold, from the cherry tree boughs.

John laughed. "Thanks, but I'll pass. I might never get out of the thing. Your back garden is spectacular. It looks like a jungle. I love the pond and the bridge. And what's the little cottage for?"

"It's my studio. Where I write." My first blind date after my divorce was with a down-on-his luck carpenter who'd built yachts in his heyday. He'd lost that job because of his nose and what he sniffed into it. He was more or less clean and sober by the time I met him. I hired him to design and build the studio when I realized the B&B would potentially be crowded with guests. The romance, like most of my romances, skidded to a jarring halt when he proved to be surly in the morning, bad tempered by afternoon, and miserable by nightfall. My track record with men was one of the reasons my nieces had labelled me *Catch and Release.*

"What's the square footage on the studio?"

Damn. I'd have to make up a list of guest's questions and find reasonable answers for them. But now all I could do was tell the truth. "I'm not sure, but it has plumbing and a loft." And the interior had rounded corners with built-in ship's storage, and the most ingenious little galley. It was the perfect marriage between a boat and a cottage.

"Maybe I could have a look? I'm interested in innovative housing."

"Sure. I'll let you get settled first. Your bathroom's just down the hall. If you want a beer or some tea, come on down, and then I'll show you the studio."

"Thanks. Oh, if I'm late tonight and you're out, do I need keys?"

I hadn't thought of that either. I only had one set.

"Oh, no problem," I lied. "I never lock the doors."

"In Vancouver? You're a trusting soul."

"It's all in the energy you send out," I babbled. "Like attracts like."

Get extra keys made, I added to my mental to-do list.

The next morning, I was up at five after a mostly sleepless

night spent radiating fearful energy that could have attracted every serial killer in the city. Unlocked doors, indeed.

John had said he'd like breakfast at seven because he was hitting the links early. I knew he drank coffee, but I hadn't thought to ask him what he might like to eat. In a nervous frenzy, I made fruit salad, currant scones, and blackberry muffins. I hadn't mentioned on the website that I was a vegan vegetarian, figuring it would limit my clientele. I had no intention of allowing bacon into my pristine kitchen, but now I was worried about that decision—this was a husky Canadian man who looked like he ate substantial quantities of animal protein.

Buy bacon at the same time as keys, I added to my to-do list. To hell with purism, where had it ever gotten me? Quantity—that was probably the answer for now. Load the table and he'd never notice the missing animal protein.

I whipped up whole wheat pancakes, sautéed veggies for an omelette, and carefully sliced up potatoes to sauté in butter. I unthawed homemade baked beans, put on a pot of coffee, and put oranges through the juicer. I raced out to the garden and picked pansies for a centerpiece and basil leaves to garnish the eggs.

When he came down the stairs at 6:47 a.m., the table was a work of art, the kitchen was a colossal disaster, and I'd sweated through two Gap tees. Nevertheless, I greeted him as if I'd spent the morning sipping café au lait whilst painting my toenails.

I seated him in the dining room and poured coffee and juice, wading through the mess in the kitchen to even reach the stove.

"This can't all be for me." He stared at the baskets and plates and hot and cold entrees. "I usually just have a bowl of cold cereal. Maybe that and a piece of toast?"

"No problem. Whole wheat or white?"

Two slices of toasted white bread and a bowl of Cheerios later, he reached for a muffin as I poured him another coffee.

"You been doing this B&B thing long?"

Busted.

"Nope. Just starting." I collapsed across from him and sipped my green energy drink, hoping it would revive me enough to make quasi-intelligent conversation. "What sort of work do you do, John?" Get him talking, that was the ticket.

"I'm the mayor of a small town on the Island."

He named it, and I barely managed to swallow without choking. Even I'd heard about this idyllic little community. There'd been a glowing article in *Vancouver Life* announcing that his town had won an award from the Planning Institute of British Columbia for innovative housing. The reporter extolled its bucolic charms and smart leadership. And here I was entertaining the mayor, for God's sake. Right here in my own dining room. Me, a political imbecile who didn't even vote. I racked my brain for a suitable conversational lead, grateful I'd used cloth napkins and my best china.

"Is this your first, um, term?" Is that what they called it?

"Nope. I've been mayor since 1992."

"Do you have to—" Here we were again. I couldn't think of the word for convincing people to vote for you.

"Campaign?" He shook his head and munched on my humble muffin. "I've never campaigned. I've been lucky enough to be elected by acclamation. But I'm getting to be too much of a fixture, so it's probably time for me to step down and let someone else take over."

"Did you always want to be a—" Politician? Boss of a town? It came to me, thank heaven. "—elected representative?"

He laughed. "Not in my wildest dreams. See, I started out as a junk collector."

This was amazing. I abandoned my herbal tea and leaned forward, elbows on the table. "How did you make the transition?"

"It just happened." He shrugged. "I hated school, quit in grade ten. I started working for a contractor cleaning up after the workmen, driving his truck to the dump and back. I saved my money and bought a beat up half ton of my own, started cleaning up after a couple of other contractors. Then I bought another truck and hired my cousin. One thing led to the next. I bought a big truck, then another. Hired more relatives and friends. Eventually, a garbage contract came up for the town. I bid on it. I didn't get it that year, but I did the next. I formed a company."

"And then what?" I poured more coffee, hoping he'd finish the story before he ran off to play golf.

"I believed in being fair. I always gave my employees the chance to buy into the business. Most of them have been with me since the beginning. I had ups and downs, but I eventually got the garbage contracts for most of the towns in B.C. Then one of my employees decided I should run for town council when a situation came up that we all felt was unfair. There was a lot of apathy going around. I got in, did that for a couple of years before the town was incorporated. I found out how things work on the municipal level. See, everybody complains about government, but the only way to change things is to get in there and do it yourself. I made some changes when I got elected, and now our little town does pretty well."

"What sort of changes?" I was really into this conversation. I reached for a muffin and buttered it, and sure enough he took a second one.

He bit into it, and after he'd swallowed he said, "Oh, first thing I did was close down the municipal offices. What did we need all that space for? It cost the town a fortune. Now we use the church if we need to have a meeting. Otherwise, everybody runs things out of their homes. It made for substantial savings and we funded a much needed community daycare centre with the money we saved. It operates out of our old building."

"What else?" I was making mental notes. This guy was a

ringer for a romance hero.

"I got the council going on affordable housing. I knew enough about the building trades to know that it was possible to design and build a pretty nice three-bedroom house for $160 thousand. We've put up seven houses so far and there's another four starting. We're pretty careful who we sell to. We've paid for the land by throwing a series of charity golf events and fishing derbies." He swallowed the last of his muffin and drained his coffee mug. "Speaking of golf, I've got to get a move on. The mayor of Vancouver and I are teeing off in half an hour." He got to his feet.

"Thanks for a great breakfast. Sorry I didn't eat more."

The man was an entrepreneur, the first I'd ever met. I might never have such an opportunity again.

"What suggestions do you have for me, John?" I babbled, all but clutching at his shirt front. "I'm just starting out and I really need feedback."

He paused at the bottom of the stairs. "You're doing great. You're going to be a big success at this B&B thing. The house is just eccentric enough and so are you."

Me, eccentric? I opened my mouth to say a dubious thank you, but he was on a roll.

"You have a knack for making people feel at home, you obviously like to cook, and the bed is really comfortable. And you're an excellent listener. Play up the romance writer thing, folks are fascinated by that. There are a couple things you could do to improve business, though."

"What?" I'd asked for it. I steeled myself for painful criticism.

"How many bedrooms do you have for guests?"

"Three."

"At the price you're charging, that's not enough to make a hefty profit on the venture." He jabbed a thumb in a westerly direction. "There was an old gent walking around your garden at two this morning calling for somebody named Sammy."

My neighbour. I should have guessed. John was going to suggest muzzling the old man. I'd grown so used to Louie wandering around my garden searching for his tomcat I never heard him anymore and hadn't thought to warn my guest about his nocturnal wanderings.

"Sorry, that's Louie Price. He's seventy-six, mentally challenged, and his only companion is his ginger cat, Sammy. He has a caregiver, but he's alone at night. Louie gets nervous when Sammy stays out late."

"Well, not to sound ghoulish, but Louie is a certain age. When and if his house comes up for sale, I'd buy it the moment it hits the market. You don't have enough bedrooms here to really make serious money, and you could turn the one next door into rooms with ensuites. Knock the fence down and run the two places together with a covered walkway."

He was on a roll. "Get your gardener to marry up the two areas. In the meantime, I'd knock out that wall—" he said, gesturing at the one separating my bedroom from the dining room. "Expand the dining room, incorporate the deck by adding one of those Plexiglas enclosures. Charge extra for serving breakfast in the tree house." With another one of those engaging grins, he headed up the stairs, leaving me to tackle the mess in the kitchen and mull on the vast chasm between genius—John—and mediocrity—me.

The space in between had everything to do with the size of one's dreams. So, B&B entrepreneur, dream big!

BLUE COLLAR CREATIVE MUFFINS
(John liked these)

Preheat oven to 350°F

Mix together:
2 eggs
½ cup vegetable oil
¾ cup brown sugar
½ teaspoon vanilla

In a separate bowl, sift together:
2 cups unbleached flour
1 teaspoon baking powder
½ teaspoon salt

Choose any <u>one</u> of the following to add to your wet stuff, and keep in mind the basic ingredients do not make edible muffins without some of this stuff added.

2 cups grated apples and 1 teaspoon lemon peel
or

1 ½ cups mashed bananas plus ½ cup chocolate chips
or

1 ½ cups blueberries, blackberries or whatever you have, fresh, frozen or dried, plus 1 tbsp. good old grated lemon peel
or

1 ½ cups dried cranberries plus (you guessed it) lemon peel

Stir dry into wet until just combined. You can add ½ cup chopped nuts to any of the above. Spoon into muffin cups (12 large) and bake for 25 minutes.

HE SEEMED LIKE SUCH A NICE MAN

By the time two weeks had passed, I figured I was really catching on to the B&B thing. I'd had four guests after the mayor—young couples in Vancouver to attend a folk music festival. They loved the massive breakfasts and by the rhythmic thumping of the beds overhead and the telltale stains on my sheets, they'd enjoyed their stay.

How does one get semen stains out of flannelette, anyway? I checked out Google. Rub with liquid soap, scrub with a toothbrush, and discard brush afterwards. Tip number one on how to run a successful B&B.

The Seattle couple arrived the following day.

"I'm Carol," she said, "and this is my companion, Lionel." They were somewhere in their late forties, laden down with three overnight bags each when they arrived at my door.

Carol was beautiful. She had masses of messy auburn curls swept carelessly into an updo, and the first eyes I'd ever seen that were honestly violet and lashed to the max. She had a lush Renoirish body that declared sexuality and she had a powerful magnet of a smile.

Lionel was five ten, large boned bordering on fat. He had a huge square head, too much straight brown hair, a vague expression on his face, and close together, washed out blue eyes that didn't quite meet mine. And his handshake was tepid and damp.

Not your Type A kind of hero, I assessed. His first words were, "Anywhere I can plug in my laptop?"

I showed them to their bedroom, pointed out the outlets, and gave them a house key and my now-familiar speech about tea downstairs whenever they were settled, with a few words about harmless Louie wandering the premises in the middle of the night calling for his cat.

Carol came down after an hour. She tucked her bare feet under her on the sofa and accepted the green tea and oatmeal cookies I offered. I asked the usual questions: who, what, when, where, and how.

Carol was a florist. Lionel—big surprise—did something obscure with computers and worked from home.

"He's really reclusive, doesn't relate well to people, but he's great when you get to know him," Carol said.

They'd met through an online dating service, had been together two years, and things were going well. Carol had been married, Lionel not.

"My first husband left me when I needed an ileostomy for Crohn's disease. He said it made him sick to his stomach. It was a blessing, because he was abusive. Physically and mentally."

"Well, good riddance to him." I told her I'd had a husband like that. Well, two of them, actually. As for the ileostomy, I'd written eight medical romances and some of the research actually stuck to my slippery brain. Ileostomy—surgical creation of an opening called a stoma from the small intestine to the abdominal wall. The colon and rectum are either removed or bypassed. Digestive wastes are expelled via the stoma into a bag. Not what every little girl dreams of having when she grows up. I studiously avoided glancing at the affected area.

"That must have been so hard for you, that operation." I felt such compassion for her. Aging was hard enough without nasty holes showing up where they weren't intended.

She nodded and nibbled on an oatmeal cookie. "After I got

out of the hospital, I made detailed plans on how to kill myself," she said candidly. "I stockpiled pills and bought old fashioned straight razors at garage sales and learned about cutting lengthwise rather than across. But then I decided to go out on one more date before I did it. Just to confirm that I was now going to totally disgust every single man alive."

"And what happened?"

She giggled. "This guy I knew took me out to dinner and I waited until we'd had dessert to explain in great detail about the stoma and the bag, and he listened and then all he said was, *Is it catching*? When I said no, he came on to me."

I laughed with delight. There was hope for the male species.

She went on.

"Almost the same thing happened with three other guys over the next six months, and it finally dawned on me that all they cared about was that there was still a nice warm place to put it, and they couldn't catch whatever I had."

We giggled at the beguiling simplicity of men.

"So you gave up on suicide and decided to be promiscuous instead?" I said, summing it up for her.

"You got it." She wrinkled her pretty nose. "It's way more fun than suicide. And besides, I figured my life was spared once already, so I had an obligation."

"The operation. Yeah, that must have been so scary."

"Well, that too, but I meant one other time. See, when I was in college, I dated a serial killer."

"Omigod. Who?"

"Gerard Schaefer. I met him in college in Fort Lauderdale. I dated him for about two months, but there was something not right about him, so I dumped him."

"Good instincts." I added that I hadn't heard of him.

"He went to church. He became a cop, of all things. He was convicted of torturing and killing two young girls, but it's pretty certain he killed as many as thirty, some right about the time I knew him. And like everyone says about Jeffrey Dahmer, Gerard seemed like such a nice guy and was fairly good looking. He was a good kisser, I remember that."

We both shuddered.

"Do you have nightmares over it?"

"I used to, while he was still alive. But he was stabbed to death in prison in 1995. It made me doubt my taste in men, that's for sure."

"But now you have a good one?" I tried to sound positive. Lionel hadn't struck me as a romantic hero.

"Oh, I really do. Lionel is a super guy. He's a bit eccentric. All he reads are murder mysteries and he's really antisocial, but I make up for it."

I wanted to ask her if Lionel had ever wet the bed, killed small animals, and lit fires, but I held my tongue.

That night, I slid a heavy chest in front of my bedroom door and slept with scissors under my pillow. Sometimes that damned theory about energy and like attracting like is no comfort at all. The lesson here for the discerning, discreet B&B hostess is to install a really good lock on the bedroom door, just in case. There's that famous line about trusting in God and tying up one's camel.

Blue Collar B & B

BLUE COLLAR OATMEAL-CHOCOLATE CHIP SERIAL COOKIES
(Because you can't stop at only one)

Cream together:
1 cup soft butter
1 cup white sugar
1 cup brown sugar

Add:
2 teaspoons vanilla
2 tablespoons milk
2 eggs
Beat well

In a separate bowl, sift:
2 cups flour
1 teaspoon salt
1 teaspoon baking powder
1 teaspoon baking soda
Stir into creamed mixture.

Add:
2 ½ cups oats
1 ½ cups chocolate chips
Walnuts or pecans

Roll into golf ball size balls, flatten with fork, bake at 350°F for about 14 minutes.

WOULD YOU FOR A QUARTER? WOULD YOU FOR A MILLION?

It was shortly after my encounter with the serial murderer's ex-girlfriend that I learned an important lesson about economics.

Cameron, a handsome gentleman of a certain age, came to stay for three days. He was a businessman, semi-retired, but in demand as a mentor. He was the keynote speaker at a conference being held at a downtown hotel. We were contemporaries, and over breakfast that first morning I learned that he read widely. We discussed Cormack McCarthy and Oliver Sacks, and I totally forgot to serve the pan fried potatoes.

Most of the men I'd met recently flipped through news magazines and pored over trade publications, so Cameron was a novelty. He actually asked if he could borrow one of my romances. I gave him one and signed it.

He had a wicked sense of humour, his own teeth, and quite a lot of hair (no comb over). He wasn't even a recovering alcoholic. He had a wife in eastern Canada—he said they were living apart, a *trial* separation.

The second morning he asked if I'd go to dinner with him that evening. I did, wearing a slippery, sexy black sundress, my rose pashmina shawl, and new Italian high heeled sandals—he was three inches taller than my five ten, and wearing heels without towering over a man was a luxury for me.

We dined at a seafood restaurant on Granville Island, talking non-stop over salmon, sipping exquisite wine, admiring a red and orange sunset reflected in the high-rise windows across the water. We walked the pier, laughing at the cheeky gulls. There were three street musicians playing on the wharf, and he waltzed me up and down, oblivious to the horrified giggles of teens grouped at a wooden table outside a pub. We dropped into Death By Chocolate, a take-out dessert paradise, where the choices included Between the Sheets, Latin Lover, and Crumble In My Arms. He insisted on buying me a huge assorted box of their best dark. We went home after that. Inside the door, he took me in his arms and kissed me. He was a great kisser and he didn't remind me at all of Jeffrey Dahmer.

"Do you enjoy sex?" he asked in a husky whisper.

Of course I did. What's not to enjoy?

"Would you consider spending the night with me?"

I thought about it for three seconds and agreed. I figure once a single woman passes fifty, the number of sexual propositions diminish. For the first forty years or so, there's an overabundance of choice. After that, whenever opportunity presents itself, go for it, I say. Love the one you're with, as the song suggests. How do we ever know when it's the last time we have the chance to be made love to by anyone besides ourselves? And I had that box of condoms. Did condoms have a best-before date?

But the following morning, I really hoped I'd get another shot at copulation before I died because it had been more than a little disappointing with Cameron. In spite of using every trick I'd ever heard of and a few I made up on my own, Cameron couldn't go the distance. He had a terminal case of premature ejaculation, which he really didn't want to talk about. He ignored the whole fiasco, murmuring (incredibly) how wonderful it had been for him—all fourteen seconds of it. I did ask him what his sex life was like with his wife, and he said it was pretty much non-existent; she'd never liked it. I believed him. I mean, what was in it for her? He was a lovely man, but he needed intensive therapy.

Cameron left the next morning, and I gave him back the money he paid me for accommodation. How could I charge him? I thought of billing him for only one night, but that seemed tawdry. For about five minutes, I considered charging him triple for the second night. But I reluctantly came to my senses. A quarter or a million, if you accept money, it's still a business transaction.

A few days later he sent me two dozen long stemmed red roses. I have the worst damned luck with roses. For the first day, these were glorious, and I did everything anyone ever suggested to get them to open—cutting off stems at an angle, soaking in warm water in the bathtub, adding plant fertilizer and aspirin. As usual, however, they started to droop that first night, and after the third day when petals were dropping everywhere, I threw them out.

Even I could see the analogy.

Alas, the discerning hostess should resist any and all overtures regarding seduction. Don't sleep with the clients. It's economic suicide. And if you absolutely can't resist, remember that there's no way of telling beforehand whether or not the roses are going to go the distance.

ROSE HIP TEA

You can wait till fall, pick the rose hips(ruining your manicure) and dry them and then soak them and make tea, but I'd just go out and buy a box of Celestial Seasonings.

NEVER LOOK A GIFT HORSE

"So," said Eric, red biking helmet and wide white smile firmly in place. Eric is my dear friend. He's a dental mechanic, constructing and repairing dentures, crowns and bridges. He's the best in the city. His teeth are always spotless, although the rest of him isn't usually.

He rides his bike everywhere, and wears his helmet ninety percent of the time he's not riding his bike. Don't ask, I don't know. It's not because he's bald; he has a thick head of straight black oriental hair moulded permanently to the shape of his helmet. And right now he was in full throttle, fairly vibrating with excitement.

"So, *sooooo,* this guy who stayed here was a documentary filmmaker?"

I'd already told him five times that yes, Josh Gilbert stayed at the B&B, and yes, he was making a documentary film about Tommy Chong, the dubiously famous comedian, marijuana activist and former half of the comedy team Cheech and Chong. And yes, yes, yes, Josh and I hit it off. We *got* each other, in some obscure retro-reincarnational fashion.

When something catches his interest, Eric extracts detail after minute detail. I've told him he'd make a perfect dentist. It's also crossed my mind that Eric and Louie have this trait in common, this single-minded insistence on repetition. Eric interrupts any attempt at changing the subject, asking the same question fourteen thousand different ways just in case I've forgotten to include something. After a while, I'd say anything to get him to stop the inquisition. Louie doesn't do the fourteen thousand different ways. He sticks to simple, endless repetition of the same statement.

"So what's he like, Josh Gilbert?"

I know Eric is fascinated because he, too, is a photographer and would love to make documentaries. But we've also exhausted this route already. I sigh and try for new adjectives.

"Intense, good looking, off-the-charts smart. About your age."

Eric was forty-eight.

"Shy, attractive, sexy, doesn't eat, lives on caffeine. Compulsive, driven, I'd guess mega-talented. Chakras amazingly open, still excited by everything. He's writing, directing, and filming the whole thing about Tommy Chong by himself, which is so brave. He's polite, humble in a sort of brashly endearing New York way."

"A famous filmmaker from New York," Eric sighs. "And you asked him to leave when he wanted to stay on?"

"I had to. He reserved for only two nights and I was fully booked for the third."

"And he filmed you."

"Yeah, even though I told him I'm the least photogenic person in the western world. I sat on a chair in the garden and he asked me questions about life and death and food and destiny. In relation to Tommy Chong."

"But you don't even know Tommy Chong. You never met him, right?"

"Right. I told Josh that, too." I was raising babies and trying to survive several desperate and abusive marriages during the sixties and early seventies. I remembered those years all too clearly, which of course means I didn't partake in sex and drugs and rock and roll.

Blue Collar B & B

"I mostly just babbled on about spirituality."

Eric shook his head. "You know, you have spiritual Tourette's. What did you tell him, all that stuff about there only being one of us here and God didn't make this world, we did, and it's all a dream anyway, that we're actually safe at home and not here at all?"

"Yup." Eric makes me laugh, which is why I love him. In the midst of the relentless questioning, he'll come up with some off the cuff insightful remark like that spiritual Tourette's line—which isn't accurate, not really. I never launch into my spiritual beliefs unless someone asks me what they are. Of course, I'm very good at getting people to do that.

I also love Eric's generosity, his kindness, his refusal to criticize. He never refuses anything lest he hurt someone's feelings. He always says *thanks, maybe later* when I offer him food he doesn't want to eat. And I love that he can fix almost anything, and does so at my beck and call, even when toilets bung up or something electrical goes haywire. And he's endlessly patient with Louie, who is the bane, and thus the blessing, of my existence.

As I said before, Louie is mentally challenged and his major, endless, single-minded topic of conversation is his ginger tomcat, Sammy. That is, when he's not trying to convince me he used to be a fashion photographer who filmed women in their underwear, or explaining that the cat actually owns my property.

More of Louie later, right now there's Eric and the black garbage bags of gifts he leaves on my back deck several times a week, always in the middle of the night. I sleep as if I'm comatose. I never hear Eric come into the garden, or creep up the steps and steal away again, but when I open the deck curtains in the morning, there'll be a bag of the most astounding stuff—hundreds of CDs, boxes of luxury soap, bottles of shampoo, obscure magazines, dozens of pens and pencils, pirated movies, books, and once a heavy, white embroidered silk, authentic

Japanese kimono complete with obi belt. It fit me perfectly; where I'd ever wear it, though, was anybody's guess. Well, I guess if I ever wanted a traditional Japanese style wedding, it would be perfect. It's sure not something you lounge around in while watching Oprah and eating microwave popcorn.

I know Eric gets the loot from Dumpster Dan, a tall, dark, tragically beautiful alcoholic who makes his living scavenging garbage cans on the wealthy end of town late at night. Dan's a refugee from some Eastern bloc country, in Canada without official sanction. The word is he murdered someone from his hometown. Or maybe several someones, but after the first one, it's just a matter of numbers. He lives in a basement room so crowded with his dumpster treasures there's barely room to move. But then again, so does Eric.

He and Eric have some unfathomable agreement about the merchandise Dan gathers. Eric gets his pick, but I know him well enough to understand that whatever it is he does in return for Dan repays him a thousand fold. Maybe it's a tooth thing?

I try to thank Eric for my dubious largesse, but he gives me this inscrutable Chinese sidelong glance and a shy smile. I've never asked him not to keep gifting me with wild things because after I divorced, I felt like a fire that had burned dangerously low because no one cared enough to throw on another log. So I asked humbly in my prayers that someone—anyone—spoil me. Just a little.

I longed for flagons and apples and purple silk, for flowers and zircons and pomegranates and magazines and book of the month selections from Reader's Digest. I didn't want the burden of a beloved along with the largesse, I reminded the Holy Spirit respectfully. For me, men came with too much baggage. Not their baggage—mine. Until I figured out why I kept attracting good-looking abusive alcoholics, I only wanted the trappings of adoration. With its usual batty sense of humour, the universe sent Eric, and these endless, outrageous, unpredictable, late night gifts. And I am grateful. I am so grateful, because along with the wacky things he brings me is this profound connection between us, this purely platonic brotherhood, like an umbilical cord of friendship stretched between him and me. I trust Eric. I love him. Sure, he drives me nuts—but what are good friends for?

He's quiet for a while, mourning the fact that he didn't get to meet Josh Gilbert before I kicked him out. Then he perks up.

"So who's coming next?"

"A family from France. Their kid, Pierre, is here going to school at Langara College. He came by, looked at the rooms and asked if his mother, her boyfriend, his sister, *her* boyfriend, and his uncle could come and stay for a week. You have to come by and meet them."

"Wow. Full house."

"Yeah. It's gonna be fun."

"Do they speak English?"

"I hope so, because I only had two years of French at school, and I flunked. All I remember is: *J'entre dans la salle de classe. Je regarde autour de moi, je dit bonjour au professeur.*"

"Quelle horrible," Eric pronounced.

The next morning on the deck, a black plastic bag wrapped around a narrow box revealed a full set of educational tapes. Conversational French, straight from Berlitz. I guess the message here is, *Don't be careful what you ask for.* Just expect it, be grateful and then duck, because sure as hell it's coming down the tube.

PAIN PERDUE OR LOST BREAD
(The original French name for French toast)

Preheat a griddle to good old moderate.

Beat 3 eggs severely

Add:
(omigod) 3/4 to 1 cup of sugar

Beat again

Dissolve 1 tablespoon cornstarch in a little water and beat that in

Beat in:
1 cup whole milk or cream
½ teaspoon nutmeg

Coat 6 slices of stale white bread
(Homemade is superb; if bought, French loaf style works.)

Butter hot griddle, add bread and cook 3 or 4 minutes on each side. Serve hot with maple syrup or berry sauce.

Send guests out for a nice long walk to counteract the effect on their blood sugar.

A RAT BY ANY OTHER NAME

Monique, Alphonse, Lulu, Gerard, and Monique's bachelor brother, Henri, arrived the following afternoon, and I got them settled in their respective rooms. Their English was on a par with my French, but fortunately Pierre was able to translate, at least for the first hour. Then he left for classes and I was on my own.

By now, I had a printed sheet with my Blue Collar logo welcoming guests with a checklist of what they preferred for breakfast. After French toast, pancakes, or Irish oatmeal, I'd coyly added this: *Something wonderful at the cook's discretion.* They all checked that one, making me curse myself—who knew I'd have to come up with something suitable for jaded French palettes?

There was a rapid-fire exchange over which beverages they wanted. Juice, yes, coffee, yes, but could I also make them *chocolat?* With a smile and exuding confidence I was far from feeling, I said, "Absolutely." I had no idea what true French *chocolat* consisted of, but I was fairly certain Fry's Cocoa wasn't going to cut it.

Good old Google found me a recipe. A call to Starbucks revealed that the special chocolate I needed was at Superstore, in the bulk section. I picked it up along with several quarts of whipping cream, cooked up the basic recipe, and the next morning concocted cups of thick, sinfully rich *chocolat,* complete with whiffs of cinnamon on top. I basked in their effusive French praise.

Henri, who'd been flirting mildly with me ever since I'd told Pierre that yes, I was single, threw me an extravagant five finger kiss, and the others pronounced breakfast très, très, très bien.

Having guests for longer than one or two mornings was challenging. I didn't want to serve the same thing every day, so each night I pored over cookbooks, trying to come up with new and exciting offerings, which necessitated ever earlier mornings for me.

Crawling out of bed at five to have breakfast ready for eight, I made cheese and tomato pie, egg nests, and quiche. I even went totally berserk and started setting dough at night for fresh croissants.

In true French fashion, my guests were up to the challenge. Breakfast became a feast, with everyone tasting, commenting, approving. Henri had progressed to kissing my hand, encrusted though it was with flour, butter, spatters of egg, and flecks of chocolate.

Then on the fourth morning, as I was sautéing zucchini for an omelette, Henri crept down the stairs before anyone else was up, and with a wink and a bent forefinger, invited me to follow him. He was wearing blue and white striped pajamas, and his fly was gaping. I tried not to look, but I am insatiably curious. Not that I was attracted to Henri. His sister and I had learned to communicate, as any two sensible women will do, and she'd confided that Henri had been married three times, that all the women had left after only a few months, that he was intolerably fussy, slept with an eye shield and ear plugs, and couldn't tolerate anyone in his bed for longer than half an hour. I thought she'd hinted at some fascinatingly obscure sexual deviation as well, but the language barrier was too extreme for me to get the real gist of it.

I gestured at the sauté pan, but he was insistent. What

the hell. It was flattering that he found me attractive, and I could gently disengage myself after he'd made his initial move. It seemed easier than standing in the hall arguing. I turned off the stove and followed him up the narrow staircase.

Henri was in the gabled room at the front of the house. He took my hand and led me into the bedroom, closing the door firmly behind us. I waited for him to put his arms around me. Instead, he gestured down at the rug. Chunks of beige carpeting were strewn everywhere. The rug had been chewed all along the doorsill.

"Un rat," he whispered. "Un grand rongeur." He made rapid chomping motions with his teeth, but I understood his French. Rat was rat in any language.

Totally horrified, I stared down at the mess. "It must have been trying to get out," I whispered. My skin crawling, I glanced at the ill-fitting doors that led to the closets and the crawl space under the eaves. Monsieur Rat had to still be in there. This bedroom and the adjoining spaces were self contained. What if the thing had bitten Henri? Images of bubonic plague and massive lawsuits swirled in my head.

"Oh, Henri, je suis regret," I stammered. "Je suis très— devastated. So, so sorry."

Henri shook his head, held out his hands and raised his eyebrows in a quintessential French gesture. I took it to mean, what can anyone do? Monsieur Rat was obviously an act of God.

Downstairs, a glance at the clock showed that it wasn't yet seven. Regardless, I picked up the phone with trembling fingers and dialled.

"Eric? Oh, God, Eric, there's a rat in the upstairs bedroom."

Silence. Breathing. I'd woken him up.

He cleared his throat. "So, Henri came on to you, huh? I figured you couldn't trust him." He'd met my guests and liked them, reserving judgment only on poor Henri.

"It's a *rat*, Eric. As in rodent. It's no joke. What if they report me to somebody?"

"Like the Rat Patrol?" He let out an amused snort and then coughed and cleared his throat. "Okay, what time is breakfast over with?"

"Ten."

"I'll ride over on my lunch hour."

He arrived at noon with four rattling rat traps looped around his neck, tied together with shoelaces so he could carry them on his bike. He made his clanking way upstairs and crawled into the spaces between the walls and carefully baited the traps with peanut butter. I hovered in the bedroom doorway, ready to make a quick run for it if Monsieur Rat made a break for freedom.

"These traps are big," Eric warned, crawling backwards out of the closet. "It's gonna make an awful noise when the rat gets caught." He was sweating profusely. "If it happens at night, it'll wake everybody up because the trap will snap and the rat will squeal."

I shuddered. "And I'll phone you to come and get rid of it."

He gave a wicked grin. "Henri can do it. It's in his room, it's his rat."

The French were with me for another three days and I didn't have another room for Henri unless I invited him to share my bed, which I wasn't about to do, rat or no rat. Amazingly, he didn't ask to be moved, but Monique did tell me he stopped sleeping with ear plugs.

I lay awake at night praying the trap wouldn't go off. I spent the days like a zombie, praying it would. I racked my brain for ways to get my guests out of the house early each morning so they'd avoid the death screams when the rat hit the trap. So, I foolishly offered to teach them Canadian softball, ignoring the fact that I hadn't played since elementary, and had forgotten or probably never learned the rules of the game, being the antithesis of a team player, or an athlete. I led the way to a nearby playing field and made up my own totally civilized version. One base only. The person at bat had as many tries as he wanted to hit the ball. If anyone out in the field got tired or bored, he or she could put up their hand and the entire group had to take a break. There was no winning or losing, just the playing of the game. Every twenty minutes or so, we paused for the orange juice liberally laced with wine I'd brought along.

They loved it all, and for a few glorious hours, I even forgot about the rat. Home again, I sent up a fervent prayer that the thing had died in one of the traps while we were out.

My guests went out for dinner, and Eric wheeled into the back garden soon afterward to check the trap line.

"Nothing," he said, sweating under his bike helmet as he emerged from the nether regions of the attic. "But there's a whole pile of shells up there from those pistachio nuts you have in each bedroom."

I'd graced each room with a bowl of pistachios and another of chocolate in case my guests needed a snack. The nuts had been disappearing at a phenomenal rate.

"Can rats shell pistachios?"

Eric shrugged. "They're pretty smart. They must have, or where did all the shells come from?"

"Then maybe we should use pistachio nuts instead of peanut butter in the traps?"

Eric gave me a look. "Have you ever tried to set a rat trap? Even with peanut butter, you ought to insure your fingers." He held up a hand, encased in a heavy leather glove. "There's no way to get a pistachio nut to stay under the spring."

"Okay, but how come the thing isn't getting caught if peanut butter's so great?"

"It will. There's lots of poop in the crawl space, so we know he's around." He grinned, white teeth gleaming. "Maybe you've got the only rat in Vancouver that's allergic to peanut butter."

"Don't joke. This isn't funny. I can't sleep and I'm terrified of being sued over rat bites. If there's one rat, there's bound to be more."

But nothing happened, although the last two nights the French were there, I barely slept, wondering where the rodent was and what it was doing. By the morning of their flight back to Paris, Monsieur Rat was still at large and I was seriously sleep deprived.

The moment came for departure. They each gave me a resounding kiss on each cheek, a substantial tip, and a barrage of French I took to mean they'd enjoyed staying in spite of acts of God. And the moment they were in their taxi, I called an exterminator, asking if they could park down the block and skulk down the alley, creeping in through my back door—the last thing I wanted was the neighbours knowing I had rats. Nosy Louie couldn't keep a secret to save his soul, and the nice people on the other side had asked about reservations for visiting relatives from Peking. I was already trying out recipes for tofu scrambler.

The gum chewing receptionist at Pestaway promised anonymity and then asked for my Visa number. This was going to cost about as much as I'd made on the French, but what else could I do? Eric, for the first time, had failed me.

Three hours later, two humourless men lumbered down the alley, covered from head to toe in white hazard suits, carrying big bulky gym bags stuffed with traps. This was their idea of discretion? They unpacked and disappeared into the crawl space. I wrung my hands in between scrubbing the bathroom and pulling the sheets off the beds, revealing that everyone except Pierre had had a rollicking good time. Thankfully, I'd saved that toothbrush.

"Ma'am?" One of the spacemen held out something in a small plastic box. "We don't think you have a rat." He gestured to the small round pellets in the box.

"This is gerbil feces and by the number of nutshells in there, you may have more than one."

Blue Collar B & B

Immediately, I thought of Norway and things became clear.

Several months before, I'd rented a room long-term to two Norwegian art students, plump pretty girls with that engaging accent, lovely skin and those soulful blue eyes. They'd asked if they could have a pet, and I'd gently refused. They'd gently gone out and bought two gerbils, which they smuggled in and kept hidden in their closet until the day I went in to investigate a strange whirring noise and found the little creatures running frantically around the wheel in their cage. I said the gerbils had to go, but I didn't have the foresight to ask exactly where they'd gone. Shortly afterwards, summer came and the girls left for home, never to be heard from again. Obviously, the gerbils were another story.

"We suggest live traps," said the exterminator. "They should be easy to catch, with the right bait."

"Which is?"

"Nuts. They love nuts."

Like pistachios. Honestly, Eric.

"How long does it take gerbils to have babies?" I had no idea if the Norwegians' gerbils were the right sexual mix, but it seemed likely the girls would have bought one of each.

"Two weeks."

I calculated how many weeks the girls had been gone and multiplied by gestation days. The numbers were staggering, even to my mathematically challenged brain. I could now have enough gerbils in my walls to supply every kindergarten class in greater Vancouver, with some left over for Surrey.

My voice wobbled. "Live traps, dead traps, poisoned pistachios, I don't care. Just get rid of them, I'm trying to run a business here." The men flinched and I realized I was shouting. So I was hysterical—I had good reason.

It took two weeks and several dozen live traps to rid my house of the pests, during which time I had to tell prospective guests that I was so sorry, but I was fully booked. And the little devils had been busy. The final gerbil head count was eleven.

They cost me loss of income, plus far more than the Norwegians and the French together had paid, but the day finally came when the rodent men declared my walls gerbil free.

I'm not exactly sure what the message is here for the B&B hostess. Don't rent to Norwegians? Beware of gerbils? Don't trust Eric when it comes to pistachio nuts? Those, certainly, but also: always expect the unexpected. The truly great thing about running a B&B is the unpredictability of events. It's similar to having someone ask what you like in bed. The answer, of course, is *surprise me*, bearing in mind that no one ever promised all surprises would be wonderful.

JUST A NOTE ABOUT BEDBUGS

Thanks be to the Universe and all the gods of hospitality, I have never encountered these nasty little morsels in my beds—but a guest from Wales did before she stayed with me. She slept at an unfortunate abode in Calgary, Alberta and was bitten. She and her friends washed every scrap of belongings and themselves before they came to me, but the bites infected and she was very ill. With the turnover of guests and the new influx of bedbugs in North America, one's chances of encountering these tiny, flat, brownish red creatures is becoming more and more likely. There are products available to get rid of them, and procedures I pray I never have to follow. Research on the Internet is enlightening. (And yes, you'll scratch for days after reading it, but as we know, everything has a consequence.)

Now, forget about that nastiness and make yourself a cup of:

Blue Collar B & B

FRENCH BREAKFAST CHOCOLAT
(As interpreted by the Blue Collar)

Into a saucepan, put:
4 squares unsweetened chocolate (Caillibot)
1 cup water
Dash salt

Stir over low heat until melted

Cook 10 minutes, stirring a lot

Cool. Fold in 1 cup whipping cream

Refrigerate

When ready to serve, put about ¼ cup in fancy mug, add hot milk to fill. Let guests sweeten to taste (or not).

LOUIE, LOUIE, OH NO, ME GOTTA GO

Having Louie creeping around the garden at 2 a.m. was certainly a surprise to my guests, and not a pleasant one at that. After he'd scared a timid little woman from England half silly, I once again tried to convince him he had to keep out of my garden.

"But I can't sleep without Sammy," Louie whined through his nose, clasping his hands over his protuberant belly, watery blue eyes magnified by his thick spectacles, bristly whiskers peppering his cheeks. He had remnants of something yellow stuck in the corners of his mouth.

"Sammy goes out at night and I worry about him."

I took several steps back, distancing myself from his potent fishy breath. I suspected he and Sammy dined on the same tins of tuna.

"I know that, Louie, but you can't wander around my garden at three in the morning calling for him. It scares my guests."

"But I need Sammy. I can't sleep without Sammy," he insisted, chin quivering.

I sighed, sorry for all of us.

"He's a tomcat, Louie. Tomcats are nocturnal." I saw the incomprehension in his eyes and amended, "They tend to wander around at night. Maybe you should lock him inside."

"Oh, no, no, I can't do that. Sammy needs his freedom, and

he thinks he owns both of our places, so he comes in your yard. He goes out his cat door, but then I need him to come home and sleep with me," Louie reiterated.

I'd had this circular conversation at least twenty-seven times in the past two months, and I should have learned by now that it never resulted in any viable solution. I'd spoken again to Louie's guardian, Caroline, and she'd promised to speak to him, as she had before. Obviously, her success rate was on a par with mine.

There were things I could do, such as call the Animal Protection people and make a complaint. There was a bylaw about animals running loose in the city. They'd come by and pick up Sammy, and it would cost Louie a considerable sum to get the cat back. After three infractions, the animal would be put down. Of course, I couldn't do that. Louie was old, and he'd lived alone since his mother died ten years ago, with Caroline watching out for him from her house across the alley. He had no immediate relatives and no friends I knew of besides me and Eric. He was lonely and mentally challenged. Bad tempered, horribly spoiled Sammy was his beloved and only companion. He'd arrived at Louie's door as a bedraggled, starving kitten that someone had dumped off, and he'd hit pay dirt. He was the old man's child in all but species.

I could choose to live trap the damned cat. Maybe being locked up for a few hours would convince him to stay within the boundaries of his own garden. But the thought of Sammy caught in the trap and caterwauling in the middle of the night was just as bad as having Louie wandering around calling for him.

"I've decided not to get married," Louie stated now, tipping his chin up and giving me a sly, rebellious look.

"Good thinking," I said, sighing, because we'd been down this rocky road plenty of times before as well. It was his usual rejoinder to my *keep Sammy in your own yard* speech, his way of letting me know that I'd had a chance at matrimony with him and had blown it.

"Women are too much trouble," he said. "It's better to just have girlfriends. I had lots of girlfriends when I took pictures of women in their underwear."

Knowing this was leading straight to some heavy breathing on his part, I headed into the house.

"Got to make an important phone call, Louie. Talk to you later."

It was hopeless. I'd just have to keep warning guests about Louie and Sammy, and apologizing when he woke them up. A few of them thought the old man and the cat added to the whacky ambience of my B&B, but I was pretty sure the majority didn't find it amusing. I certainly didn't.

Two nights later, I was jolted out of a deep sleep at 2:15 a.m. by the ringing of the telephone, the flashing of lights in the alley from the top of a police cruiser, and the frightened voices of my young guests, a honeymooning couple from Oregon. The call was from one of the cops in the alley. He confirmed my name and address, and then said, "We have a man here who insists he knows you. He was in your garden. A neighbour saw him and reported a prowler."

Louie. For just an instant I flirted with the idea of saying I didn't know him. Being taken to the cop shop would scare the bejesus out of him, and maybe he'd make more of an effort to keep Sammy at home. But I couldn't do it.

The cop said, "He wants to talk to you. Is that all right with you?"

"Put him on." Maybe I could scare the bejesus out of Louie myself, threaten him with some charge, enough to keep him and Sammy out of my yard at two in the morning.

"Bobby? It's me."

It took me a second to figure out that the frightened voice on the phone wasn't Louie's. It was Eric. "Could you come out and tell these guys I'm a friend of yours? I was just dropping by to leave you some stuff."

Blue Collar B & B

I threw on a housecoat, reassured my guests who were huddled at the top of the stairs that there was nothing to worry about and went out and confirmed to Officer Tymchuk and his good buddy that Eric was a good friend, and yes, he frequently dropped things off in the middle of the night. I could tell they were thinking hanky panky as I thanked them for their presence in the neighbourhood. When they drove off and Eric peddled shakily away on his bike, I collapsed on the back steps, still trembling from being jerked out of a rather nice dream.

"Bobby? Are they gone?"

I screamed and jumped, but it was only Louie, wearing his blue flannel pajamas with the gaping fly. He had on sporty tartan slippers, and was cradling Sammy in his arms like a baby. The lousy cat raised his head and gave me a sly look.

Louie was puffed up with importance. "Lucky I saw him, Bobby, he was sneaking up your steps. I called 911, that's what Caroline said to do if we had a prowler."

The thing was, Louie knew Eric. He was also jealous of him, as he was of any gentleman caller I had. I was pretty certain he'd known exactly what he was doing when he called the cops. The whole episode came clear to me.

I said, "So, where were you when you saw the prowler, Louie?"

Sure enough, he pointed to the end of my garden by the pond. "Sammy was over there fishing. I was trying to get him to come home to bed, wasn't I, little boy?" He tickled the cat under the chin, and Sammy hissed at him.

Mavis had just billed me for the six exotic Koi she'd brought for my pond. I eyed Sammy's bulging belly and wondered if I had any left.

"I saw him, sneaked home, and called 911," Louie declared in a triumphant tone.

"Didn't you know it was Eric?"

Louie shook his head, and then blew his defense by adding,

"He shouldn't come here in the middle of the night like that, should he?"

"Nobody should." I blew out an exasperated breath, said goodnight and went inside. Back in bed, I lay awake trying not to listen to the headboard in the upstairs bedroom banging rhythmically against the wall. My guests were consoling one another in the best possible fashion. I tried to remember which set of sheets I'd used on their bed. The flannelette set washed up easily, but I thought I'd used the high thread count silky cotton ones, which would require more pre-treatment. At least I still had that damned toothbrush.

And if there's anything to be learned from this episode, it totally escapes me.

BOBBY'S GREEN ENERGY DRINK
(For mornings after nights like the one just mentioned)

Toss into a blender in any random order:
1 banana
2 cups water
2 heaping tablespoons Hemp protein
1 tablespoon Greens
(Many different brands available,
found in health food stores)
3 tablespoons Flax oil (the high lignon kind)
And about 4 thin slices of fresh ginger.

Blend. Drink. Feel yourself becoming indomitable enough to cook breakfast. Or feed to your guests and know that whatever crap they put in their bodies after they leave your table, you've done your damndest to give them a head start towards great health and the happiness that comes from feeling good. Even if they've devoured your Pain Perdue.

OH WHERE, OH WHERE??

> *And you know that she's half crazy*
> *But that's why you want to be there*
> *(Suzanne,* by Leonard Cohen*)*

"My son's sixteen," my next guest confided. "And he's living with a woman of thirty-six. They've run off together, and I'm afraid she's on drugs. They have a three-year-old kid, my granddaughter. I need to find them. I'm worried sick about the baby."

I did the math and did a double take. Her son had fathered the baby when he was thirteen?

"What makes you think they're in Vancouver?" I poured her another coffee and sat down at the breakfast table. She was from Nebraska. She'd driven all the way to Canada with her son's battered old guitar in the trunk. She said it was his most precious possession, and leaving it behind had convinced her that maybe he hadn't wanted to run away. Maybe he'd been abducted.

She looked severely stressed: dark circles under pretty hazel eyes, stained white sweat shirt, yellow fingers from nicotine. The smell of cigarettes oozed from her pores. She'd been with me for four days, and she'd told me she was a psychiatrist. Her husband made carved wooden boxes for human ashes. She'd shown me the catalogue. The boxes were beautiful. I wasn't in the market for one at the moment, but I assured her that if the time came—.

She said, "His girlfriend's father lives here. She told me once that this is where she wants to live, too."

"Isn't it statutory rape, an older woman and such a young boy? Maybe you ought to get in touch with the cops."

She shook her head. "I don't want to get my son in trouble. He doesn't have a passport; they must have lied at the border. He'd be arrested as an illegal alien."

I had no idea if that was accurate, but I knew someone who would know. "My daughter-in-law specializes in family law. If you like, I'll call her and maybe you could talk to her."

She nodded. "Thanks. That would help."

I called, and Trudy saw my guest that very morning. She called me afterwards.

"There's something about that woman's story that doesn't sound right. I think she's a nut case. And she says her son and this older woman lived with her for six months. I ask you, what mother condones a relationship between such a young kid and an older woman?" Trudy made the sound that signifies exasperation with her. "She's fuckin' batty, you want my opinion."

The same thought had crossed my mind. "She doesn't seem the sort to go mad at night with a butcher knife, though. You figure?"

Trudy thought probably not. "Put a chair under your bedroom door just to be sure. I've got a friend on the police force, he's running her name and her son's name through the system to see what comes up."

Nothing did. The lady stayed for another four days, and the story got stranger and stranger. She said she'd visited the address she had for her son's girlfriend's father and they wouldn't talk to her.

"I have to find the baby," she kept insisting. "It's too late for my son, but that baby—I have to find my grandbaby."

The morning she was leaving, she told me her son's guitar had been stolen from the back of her car, which was parked out in

Blue Collar B & B

front of my house. I'd parked there myself for years, and hadn't heard of a single car being broken into on our street. There's always a first time, though.

Again, I said we should call the police. Again, she refused. I went out with her and looked at the car. There was no sign of damage.

"How did they get the trunk open? Usually they use a crowbar or something."

"They must have just popped it and taken the guitar."

"Was there other stuff in there?"

"Yeah, all my files, and some stuff I bought at a boutique yesterday. But they only took the guitar, which makes me think it was his girlfriend's family. Who else would do such a thing?"

I couldn't guess. It was all starting to sound more and more like the twilight zone to me. I gave her a hug, packed her a lunch, and sent her on her way with a sigh of relief. I then burned sage in every room in my house in a cleansing ceremony to rid the rooms and myself of her sad, mad energy.

I'd almost forgotten about her two weeks later when a notice came from Canada Customs. Apparently I had a parcel which required a hefty amount to be paid in duty, sent to me from Nebraska by my disturbed guest. I went to the post office and paid, expecting a small carved box in which my kids could store my ashes when the time came, although why it cost so much in duty I couldn't imagine. Maybe they'd carved it from ivory? Instead of a small box, the wooden crate was large and flat and mysterious. I couldn't wait to get it home and use my hammer on the nails.

Inside was a sizeable oil painting of a white haired woman in profile, who looked eerily like me. A note was included from the gallery that had shipped it, suggesting I insure the original piece as it was valued at well over a thousand dollars. Another note arrived several days later. My guest had seen the painting and decided to buy it for me as a token of her gratitude, because it looked like me.

All I'd done was listen to her—and agree with Trudy that she was fuckin' nuts. I felt humbled and guilty. I phoned to thank her for the amazing gift, but she wasn't there. I asked the gentleman who answered the phone to convey my thanks, and he said he would.

"She's gone off to Little Rock," he sighed.

"Did she find her son? And her little granddaughter?"

"What son?" he said in a puzzled voice. "We don't have any kids."

I mumbled something about it being my mistake and hung up.

I never saw or heard from her again.

I hung the painting on my dining room wall and guests constantly asked who the artist was who'd caught my likeness so exactly.

The Bible, in Hebrews 13:2, says, "Some have extended hospitality to angels without ever knowing it."

And some have extended hospitality to disturbed psychiatrists from Nebraska and been gifted for it. I sent her good thoughts and hoped she found whatever it was she was searching for.

CEREMONY FOR CLEANSING

It would be best to gather sage in nature, but few of us have that opportunity. This is not the domesticated, garden sage (Salvia) but rather the plants botanists identify as wormwood or mugwort, the various members of the genus Artemisia. The root syllable "art" means bear, and the bear is a universal symbol of healing.

To find the type of sage I need, I go to Banyen Books and Sound, a spiritually-oriented store in Vancouver, and buy a dried chunk, maybe 6 inches long and four inches thick. The smell of sage is the ancient smell of the earth.

Make sure you're alone—you don't want to be labelled a total nutcase. Open a window or door so that unneeded forces can find an exit. It's essential that there be a way for air to escape to the outside when you smudge. Disable smoke alarms. Light the herb with a match, and when it's caught, blow out the flames. Wave the smoke over your body. You can use your hands or the feather from a non-endangered species like a turkey or pheasant, making sure to include your arms and legs in the smoke. Turn to face each of the four directions, holding the smudge up and away from your body. Wave the smoke, saying a prayer of gratitude and healing to North, South, East and West. Offer smoke upward to the sky and downward to the earth. Imagine sunlight flooding the space.

Sounds nutty, right? But science has found smells induce altered states of awareness because of their connection with specific parts of the brain, and the ceremony allows not only the space to be purified and healed, but also one's feelings about the troubled individual.

THERE'S ONLY ONE OF US HERE

My next guest was also on a mission. Juan Sanpedro was from Madrid, a slender, strikingly handsome young man who arrived on a late flight and slept most of the first day of his visit. He surfaced late in the afternoon, and I made him coffee and toast, with a side of yogurt.

"I am here to finding a job and house," he informed me in enchanting accented English. "I will then to bring my family." He pulled out photos of them—a beautiful wife, a seven-year-old daughter, and a chubby two-year-old son, all breathtakingly attractive.

"I have make great trouble in my family, my mother and father and aunts and uncles are very much against this move," he confided, his lovely dark Latin eyes sad. "In Spain, family is everything. But Madrid, it is not safe anymore. You have heard about the train bombings?"

I didn't watch the news—I considered it group meditation on disaster—but even I knew of the horrific events of March 2004.

"I am usually on that train, but I was unwell that morning with—how do you say?" He mimed sore stomach, vomiting.

"Flu," I supplied. Fortunate flu, in this instance. "Will immigration be a problem?" I'd heard that it could be a pain in the butt.

He shook his head. "I am very fortunate. I was born in Toronto. My parents, they were touring, and poof, I decided to be born. I was two months when they take me home to Madrid, but now I have"— a small *voir dire* here as we hashed out what he intended to say—"dual citizenship," he pronounced proudly.

Juan spent five days exploring possible jobs, shipping options for furniture, real estate prices and schools. We had long discussions about families, children, finances, furniture, food, marriage, religion and the church. Juan was a Catholic atheist.

Halloween came while he was visiting, and he got right into the spirit of the thing, insisting the angels, ghosts and space creatures at my door perform a song or dance before they got their handful of miniature chocolate bars and drink boxes. Most of the kids in my neighbourhood were first generation Oriental or East Indian, just beginning to learn English, which made it doubly confusing for the poor little creatures when he tried to teach them the Spanish words for trick or treat and thank you. But with true, newly Canadian politeness, they did their best.

Juan was an interesting, exceedingly polite and colourful guest, and when he asked if I'd consider having his wife, kids and teenage sister-in-law—who was coming along to help with the children—stay with me for a short time until he found housing, I agreed, as long as my three upstairs bedrooms proved adequate.

"Si, si, perfecto," he assured me. "Muchos gracias."

We parted with a warm hug and a deep sense of friendship, but as usual, what with a steady stream of new guests and the oddities of day-to-day living, I almost forgot about Juan. Winter passed, and with spring came an email from him requesting a reservation for three rooms for several weeks. I blocked it off on my calendar.

The day of the Spanish arrival came, and with it a phone call from the airport from Juan. His English had improved about as much as my Spanish and it was tough to sort out what he was asking. It seemed that Juan had made friends on the plane with a young Spanish physician, Carlos, who was coming to Canada on a six-month exchange program to work at Children's Hospital. The doctor's accommodation plans had somehow fallen through. Would it be possible for all of them to share the three upstairs rooms, just until other plans were made? I said yes. What was one more person for a day or two, after all? But they'd have to figure out the sleeping arrangements themselves, I told Juan.

"Si, si," he assured me. "Gracias, mucho gracias."

I started having second thoughts when a limo and two oversized cabs pulled up outside. Men, women, children, a teenager, several babies and about a half ton of luggage came tumbling out. Louie came out of his house, Sammy in his arms, to goggle in amazement at the Spanish Armada. It turned out that Carlos, the doctor, had a Mrs. Carlos and a baby Carlos in tow, all of them breathtakingly beautiful to behold. But oh God, the luggage!

As a tag team, hindered by Louie and the cat, we managed to transport everything from the front sidewalk into my living room, which now overflowed with people and huge suitcases. The men set to, moving everything upstairs accompanied by rapid fire Spanish, crying babies, and much shouted encouragement—or maybe not—from the ladies.

After a while, Mrs. Carlos found a chair and settled in to nurse her baby. Juan's serious little eight-year-old daughter took charge of her baby brother. The gorgeous, languidly long-legged teenage sister-in-law went upstairs, presumably to begin unpacking, and Mrs. Juan followed the men up and down the stairs, maybe giving moral support along with rapid fire directions.

Totally overwhelmed, I stayed in the background, offering homemade soup, fresh bread and tea while wondering with a sinking heart exactly what I'd gotten myself into.

Gradually, the chaos subsided somewhat, at least until Louie came banging on the back door, supposedly looking for Sammy, but actually fascinated by the quantity of people he'd watched pour into my house. I introduced him to everyone, and they all smiled and nodded with perfect politeness and complete incomprehension as he went into his usual diatribe about Sammy's diet, bowel movements and general brilliance. Fortunately, no one could understand a word he said, and eventually I managed to nudge him out the door again.

I was afraid to even ask where the luggage had gone, much less where five adults and three children were planning to sleep. Also, three women would be sharing one bathroom, and one of them was a stranger to the other two. What if they hated one another after the first hour? They were all fairly volatile. Did my insurance cover murder?

There was also the question of food. I was a B&B, so only breakfast was on the menu. They had no transportation, and while bus service and several restaurants were only blocks away, Vancouver was in the midst of a spring downpour. Dragging tired babies out twice a day for lunch and dinner seemed inhumane, so with a few misgivings, I told Juan they could use my kitchen to prepare their meals. I was on deadline for a book, I explained, and would be spending most of my time out in my studio anyway— which was a good thing, because there was hardly any space left in the house.

During the next few days, we learned about each other's patterns, and a workable lifestyle emerged. Everyone got along, which was a blessing. I was an early riser, and all of them— including the babies—slept late, so I had a few precious hours in the morning all to myself. Breakfast for the Spanish proved a no-brainer. I prepared fresh fruit salad, set out cold cereal, yogurt and bread for toast, made some muffins or scones, set a pot of coffee to brew and left it all on the dining room table. That was that. They were *very* late risers.

From my studio, as I worked during the day, I heard their laughter and the lovely cadence of rapid, musical Spanish. It was easy to understand why it was considered a romantic language.

After breakfast every day, they went out, wandering down the street in a noisy group to the bus stop. About three, they made lunch and invariably invited me to join them, teaching me how to make a real Spanish omelette, asking the English words for real estate terms, with Juan translating. I loved having lunch prepared for me. We talked of philosophy and religion and customs and cooking.

I ate dinner at five or six and they didn't begin to consider cooking until at least nine at night. The dining room was next to my bedroom, and over the next weeks I'd be lulled into sleep by the rhythm of their soft conversation and the babbling of the children. There was always wine, and after the two babies were fed and bedded, the rest of them spent several hours over a leisurely, boozy dinner. It seemed so civilized to me, if impractical. It would make getting up early to go to work difficult.

The two weeks Juan and I had agreed upon expanded to five, and then six, as they struggled to find suitable housing in a city where prices had gone ballistic. Carlos began his stint at Children's Hospital, and he and Juan each bought second-hand cars. I introduced the women to Costco and Ikea, and inevitably, to Eric.

Eric fell head-over-heels in love with Juan's sister-in-law, who unfortunately didn't feel quite the same about him. Every morning, there was a black garbage bag on the deck with her name on it, holding bottles of perfume only slightly used, barely scratched DVDs of the current rappers, and one memorable morning, fifteen pairs of dainty high-heeled shoes, all her exact size. I tried not to feel jilted.

Carlos's adorable baby girl took her first steps on my living room carpet. Louie and Sam wandered in and out and around about, pretty much lost in the crowd. Sam took to sneaking in and sleeping on one of the upstairs beds, encouraged by Juan's sombre little daughter, who'd unaccountably fallen for the bad tempered cat.

No one was even slightly perturbed by Louie's nocturnal

wandering in the garden. The Spanish, poor trusting, misguided souls, accepted everything at the Blue Collar as their introduction to typical Canadian culture. Eventually, the day came when both couples found houses, Juan purchasing and Carlos renting. They paid me much more than I asked for, and Carlos and Juan made innumerable trips to transport the luggage and the not inconsiderable new acquisitions their wives had made at Costco and Ikea.

Juan's furniture arrived from Spain, but Carlos was trying to furnish his apartment as reasonably as possible. I took him to the Salvation Army outlet where he bought a respectable couch and two chairs, and a supply of dishes and pots and pans. Eric asked what was lacking, and the next morning we awoke to find a full set of quite good dining room furniture plus two beds on my front lawn. Eric never said where the stuff had come from or how he'd transported it on his bike, and I never asked.

On a sunny May morning, I was thoroughly kissed on both cheeks by everyone and hugged till my ribs ached. The secondhand cars drove away for the last time, and for the first time in weeks, the house was empty and silent.

I ventured upstairs. The women had done all the laundry and remade the beds. The kitchen, bathroom and bedrooms were pristine; the storage space under the sloping ceilings empty of both suitcases and—thank the lord—gerbils. They'd bought me a beautiful card and a huge salt lamp, explaining that the light it gave brought calm to any room and its inhabitants. I turned it on and cried.

Sometimes, silence is highly overrated.

Bobby Hutchinson

THE ARMADA'S SPANISH OMELETTE

Gather together in a friendly fashion:
1 cup really good olive oil
½ mild onion, chopped
5 or 6 potatoes, thinly sliced and sprinkled with salt
2 cloves garlic, chopped
5 eggs

Heat olive oil in a big frying pan.
Add potatoes carefully
Separate the slices so they don't stick together

Don't make the pan too hot.
Cook about 5 minutes, until almost soft.
Add: *garlic and onions.*
Cook another three or four minutes.
Carefully drain into a bowl, leaving some oil in pan.

In another bowl:
Whisk the eggs.
Add a little salt then pour over potatoes, stirring to coat.

Put this mess back into the frying pan, into the hot oil, covering every inch of the pan. Lower the heat and allow to cook, shaking frequently to keep from sticking, until beginning to set up (about half cooked.)

Cover the frying pan with a plate, invert the omelette and add another tablespoon of oil to the frying pan. Slide the omelette back in on the uncooked side (manual dexterity needed here.) Cook until completely set. Cut in wedges. Yummmm.

ASHES OF OLD LOVERS

With the departure of the Spaniards, it dawned on me that I had no social life of my own. I hadn't been out on a date in months, so when summer was over and my steady stream of guests slowed to a trickle, I decided to register with a Vancouver dating agency.

I met with a vivacious redhead who claimed to have set up the agency as a result of her own difficult search for a suitable partner. I assured her I wasn't in the market for marriage. I was looking for a companion, someone content enough with their own life they didn't need me to transform mine to suit them. She assured me there were plenty of guys out there of a certain age with exactly the same aspirations.

So I did the personality testing, which revealed me as an INFP—idealistic, curious, wanting to understand people and find ways of fulfilling human potential, with a high dose of stubbornness and impatience tossed in gratis. Oh, yes, and apparently I was also inclined to be impulsive. Who knew?

I supplied a flattering head shot, handed over $800, and went home to wait—impatiently—for the phone to ring. The first entry in the dating sweepstakes was Donnie. An aspiring actor, he fostered dogs for the SPCA, worked as a handyman, was divorced with two estranged daughters and a vengeful ex. He was a recovering alcoholic with a full year of sobriety under his belt. He attended AA meetings religiously.

He was of Scottish descent, wrote poetry (truly abominable, I soon found out,) and liked to wear a kilt to formal gatherings. He had a sailboat and enjoyed live theatre. He loved dining out at interesting restaurants. He confided all of this at our first meeting, a walk around a nearby park dragging a dog of uncertain origin that he was fostering.

I don't mind dogs. I've loved a few, but never owned one because keeping animals seems to me akin to being responsible for a prisoner. This dog growled low in her throat when I tried to stroke her, and so I kept my distance, sizing up Donnie while trying to keep out of the dog's way.

Donnie was considerably shorter than me, with a totally bald, tanned pate, round glasses emphasizing dancing green eyes, an actor's deep, vivacious voice, a workman's sinewy body, and the face of a wicked leprechaun. It was barely like at first sight, but, heaven help me, I decided to give it a try. He turned up for our first date with the damned dog in tow, which should have rung a warning bell.

"I'd leave her in my van, but it's cold out and she has short hair," he said in an apologetic, wheedling voice. "Do you think we could lock her in your bathroom? She doesn't bark."

I agreed, a little reluctantly. I had guests upstairs, a quiet couple from Denmark. But we were only going to a nearby movie theatre to see an experimental arts film. What could happen in two hours? We put the dog in my downstairs bathroom.

The movie was a dud, and the moment I opened my front door two and a half hours later, I could smell the dog. Or rather, the dog shit. With Donnie hot on my trail, I raced in and ripped open the bathroom door, or what was left of it, gagging at the smell as a piece of molding hit me on the head. The dog—whom Donnie belatedly admitted was part pit bull—had shit on every conceivable inch of the bathroom, including inside the tub. She'd unravelled the toilet roll, wound it around the room, and then torn off all the molding around the door. She'd chewed sizeable holes in the walls, right through the drywall to the rafters. The bathroom was a disaster area. My poor guests were traumatized—they'd barricaded themselves in their room, believing the house was being burgled by criminals with loose bowels.

"I'm sorry, I'm sorry," Donnie kept repeating as I ranted. "I'll clean everything up and repair the bathroom if you'll only let me."

Let him? What choice did I have? I wasn't about to clean up after the dog, and although Eric would probably do the repairs for me, why should he have to? It was Donnie's responsibility. It was Donnie's bloody dog. The personality test should have indicated that I sometimes make serious errors in judgment.

"I never want to see that animal again," I hissed as Donnie carried the dog out to his van. She gave me a triumphant look and growled in passing. He came back and asked for a bucket and some disinfectant.

"I'll clean this up and be here first thing in the morning with new molding and drywall," he promised. "What shade is the paint?"

"Lambskin duvet. Benjamin Moore." And fiercely expensive, I thought with malicious satisfaction.

He scrubbed and disinfected, gathered up clumps of drywall and lengths of molding while I opened windows, sprayed room deodorant and reassured my Danish guests that things were under control. When he finally left, I figured I'd probably never see Donnie again, which in retrospect might have been for the best. I knew for a fact I'd never see the Danes, but Denmark was far enough away that maybe it wouldn't hurt the Blue Collar's reputation too much.

But at nine the following morning while I was feeding my dazed guests tons of carbs to soothe their nerves, the doorbell announced his arrival. True to his word, he had everything needed to put the bathroom back together, as well as a huge bouquet of hothouse flowers for me, with a funny card that reiterated how sorry he was. It had a dog on it, which should have given me pause. He'd locked the offending animal in his van, which suited me fine.

The bathroom apparently wasn't a one day job. It dragged on, and when my dishwasher clogged up, Donnie fixed it. The flowers lasted two weeks, and then the fuel pump on my car gave up the ghost. Donnie replaced it. One afternoon while I was shopping, he ripped up the rotten boards on my deck, he said it was to prevent some unsuspecting guest falling through and suing me. I hadn't realized the flooring was that bad. Before he got around to laying new decking, he decided my back steps were unsafe, so he took them off.

The pit bull was no longer with him—unbelievably, she'd found loving parents, motorcycle types, Donnie confided. But she'd been replaced by a huge, shaggy mongrel named Charlie. While he worked, Donnie kept Charlie either locked in his van or tied on my back deck with a bucket of water and a washbasin of food.

I'd laid down the law—no dogs in my house. I asked peevishly why he couldn't leave Charlie at home, but his foster dogs all had behaviour problems, Donnie explained. His commitment was to keep them with him at all times so he could help them become more socially acceptable.

Unlike the pit bull, Charlie was overly friendly. He also had an overactive libido, and every time I got within two feet of him, he salivated and tried to mount me. I advised my guests to use the side path to the garden. All I needed was some poor innocent lady claiming she'd been raped by a dog on my deck. I was fairly certain my insurance policy didn't cover that eventuality.

As usual, I was writing a book, not paying enough attention to what was going on around me. Six weeks flew by, with two more problem dogs tied on the deck. Archie, a semi poodle, was so neurotic he'd chewed off his own fur, everywhere he could reach. He wore a cone shaped thing on his head and whined all day from frustration. The next was Bonzo, an elderly dog with a hearing problem, which meant he couldn't hear Donnie telling him to shut up, so he barked constantly.

I finished the book and woke up the next morning realizing how long Donnie and his dogs had been hanging around. The bathroom still wasn't painted, although the dry wall and molding were done. The deck was missing some flooring. The railing on the back porch was in place, but needed painting as well. While I wasn't paying attention, he'd ripped off some boards on the back fence, and it gave the garden a disreputable feeling.

The thing was, apart from the dogs, Donnie was good at being unobtrusive and helpful. He drove up every morning, had coffee and a scone, made me laugh at some anecdote usually centered around his AA meetings, and set to work. I could hear him from my studio, singing and banging away, but he seldom interrupted me. I made us lunch, and we'd often go for a walk around the park. Several times a week, he'd take me out to dinner. It was always somewhere nice. I'd sort of gotten used to having him around. But his presence was having repercussions. Eric's feelings were hurt because Donnie was doing all the jobs he usually did for me. My bags of gifts slowed to a trickle, ditto my daily phone calls from Eric's dental office. Louie complained daily and at length because Sammy was afraid of the dogs, which to me was a bonus. Anything that kept that cat from using my garden as a toilet was fine by me. But I was getting more and more nervous about the number of construction projects and their lack of completion.

I confronted Donnie one morning when I found him slapping a coat of paint, not on my bathroom or the porch railing, but on the steps leading to the deck. I'd painted those steps the year before; I didn't think they needed to be done again.

"Donnie, why isn't anything ever getting finished around here? It's starting to look like an abandoned construction project."

He used up the paint on the brush and then got to his feet, giving me a soulful look from behind his steamed up glasses.

"It's like this, see, Bobby. I'm in love with you. If I finish everything, I figure you won't go on seeing me."

I was speechless. He'd kissed me a few times, but that's as far as it had gone. He'd muttered something about a prostate operation that wasn't healed yet, precluding any sex. Not that sex and love are related, but surely falling in love should involve more than a few chaste kisses? I'd certainly banked on it, but again, writing is bad for the libido—for me at least, it uses the same energy, so for weeks I'd sort of put sex on the back burner.

Unfortunately, we weren't on the same page with this love thing. I screwed my courage to the sticking point. My nieces had labelled me catch and release for a reason, and I'd long ago perfected the ideal speech for moments like this.

Trying not to dwell on the fact that Donnie had cost me eight hundred dollars even before the renovations, I said, "Look, Donnie. You're a wonderful man, and I'm sure there's someone out there who's perfect for you, but the chemistry just isn't right between us. I'm sorry." I took a deep breath and added the part that was going to make Eric and Louie ecstatic. "I want you to pack up that dog and all your stuff and leave. Now."

He didn't argue. He slunk off with his dog between his legs, and within an hour, I was once again alone, this time with an unfinished fence, a deck missing boards, a bathroom needing paint, and sundry other small unfinished chores. I did the sensible thing and called Eric. Within a week, the jobs were completed. Eric was vindicated, Louie was content, Sammy was once again convinced my garden was his domain, and I'd learned one more lesson.

When you're a single lady running a B&B, what you need is a reliable handyman. You might also want romance—there's no reason you shouldn't have it—but combining the two is not wise. I should have remembered that church and state are never a satisfactory combination.

TIPS FOR ATTRACTING A PARTNER
(Without paying $800)

- Make a detailed list of all the qualities you desire in the OTHER.
- Make a second list of all the qualities that person would find desirable.
- The second list is the one you concentrate on.

THERE ARE NO FREE LUNCHES

The thing about a B&B is that the mattresses wear out. I imagine a well-run brothel has the same problem. Somewhere into the third year, I realized that the two double beds upstairs—which I'd bought second hand in the first place—needed new mattresses. Guests were politely hinting that everything rolled to the middle of the bed.

Eric, who doesn't believe in ever paying full price, always has a friend who has a friend. He gave me the number for a man who dealt, Eric assured me, in top quality new mattresses for a quarter of the price.

"Where does he get them from?"

"Big hotels order beds on a regular basis. He buys the overstocks."

I didn't understand how that worked, but it sounded honest enough. I was finishing a book, and hated the thought of wasting a day driving around looking for beds. Besides, who doesn't like a bargain? I called the number and a deep, lilting voice identified itself as Reuben. He assured me he'd be over in an hour.

Reuben was six feet six, East Indian, and he had tattoos down both bare, massive arms. He dipped his turbaned head under the doorjamb of my studio and dwarfed the chair I indicated for him to sit in. He dwarfed the whole damned studio. He'd have dwarfed entire provinces. His thighs were twice the size of my waist, and my waist has never been a hand span operation.

Blue Collar B & B

Through the window, I saw Louie, who'd been on his way over to interrupt me for the third time that morning, sprinting back into his own yard, Sammy tucked safely under his arm. If I was about to be mugged in my own studio by a dark-skinned giant, Louie wasn't about to save me.

"I need two double mattresses with box springs. Good quality."

"Only the best." Reuben was staring wide-eyed at the bookshelves behind me, which contained rows of my romances plus translations. "Eric, he says you write books?"

"Yeah. Would you like one for your wife?" I reached back and picked one at random. I've learned that giving someone a signed book can be great for business.

"Not my wife, no, she does not read. But myself, I would love to have one. Always, I thought how I would like to write a romance. Please, you will sign for me?"

So with heedless optimism, I wrote on the title page: *For Reuben, who will write a bestseller. Best regards, Bobby H.* There's no point ruining someone's dream by telling them that about one romance in every 4000 submissions actually makes it to print, never mind on to the bestseller list, or that a miniscule number are written by men. How did I know he wasn't the next Robert James Waller?

Reuben was overwhelmed. He stared down at the paperback, turned it over three times in his huge paw, read the dedication and clasped it to his heart. He thanked me in a trembling voice. For the next half hour, we went over how one went about starting a book, how to write outlines, where to send it, how to go about getting an agent. Finally I cleared my throat and said, "About the beds."

"Oh, the beds, yes, for you, Bobby, only the best. I will bring you tomorrow two, you will like them, you will see." He went into a technical description of chiropractic, open-coil, pillowtop whatever.

I went for the bottom line. "How much?"

"Cash, no paper?"

I agreed.

He quoted a price so low I assumed it was for only one bed.

"No, no, missus, for two. Two of my very best, only for you. And maybe I will bring you a sample of what I write, you would quickly look and tell me what you think, yes?"

What the heck. I agreed with the terms, providing he also removed the old beds and set up the new ones. I had guests arriving the following evening.

Reuben and a skinny little helper were there at noon the next day. With much hollering and what I assumed were exotic curses, they carefully manhandled the old mattresses and box springs down the narrow staircase and then reversed the operation to get the new beds upstairs—not an easy proposition. They even transferred the bedskirts and mattress pads for me.

I'd examined the beds before they unloaded them from the back of an old Ford pickup, and found them to be exactly what he'd promised—beautiful, pristine, pillowtop. Remarkable for the price.

I paid Reuben cash, and he handed me a thick sheaf of badly typed papers. His manuscript. My heart sank. I hate reading stuff and having to tell people some version of the awful truth.

"I'll read it as soon as I can," I assured him, knowing I'd put it off as long as I possibly could.

When he was gone, I went into the house, ran upstairs, and flopped down first on one bed, then the other, before I set to work making them up. They were heaven. As soon as I got my cheque for my completed manuscript, I decided, I was going to splurge and buy myself a new bed. Of course, before I could contact Reuben again, I'd have to read his writing, which sort of took the joy out of the whole endeavour.

Weeks went by. I finished the book, did the revisions, started a new outline, all the while greeting guests, cooking breakfasts, and washing sheets. Once in a while, I thought of my new bed and sighed with longing. When my book money finally arrived, I dug through the pile of paper on my desk and found Reuben's manuscript, which I hadn't yet looked at. I forced myself to take off the rubber band and skim through it. It was about as bad as I'd anticipated. The parts that were even a little good weren't original and the original parts really weren't good. The English usage was highly amusing and totally unintentional. But hey, I wasn't an editor. It took me two hours to scribble down a couple pages of honest suggestions. What they pretty much amounted to was don't quit your day job. Take an English class, or four or five. Read a few romances instead of watching the latest videos from Bollywood.

Then, dreaming of my new bed, I dialled Reuben's number.

"The number you have called is out of service," a recorded voice informed me.

I called Eric.

"Oh, yeah, Reuben," he said, with that little offhand chuckle that always signified something not good. "Reuben got arrested."

"Omigod. What for?" I started to sweat and hyperventilate. I had visions of the cops arriving tomorrow morning, ordering guests out of their lovely pillow top beds, and then reclaiming my mattresses as stolen property. And wasn't there some charge relating to receiving stolen goods?

"Well, he was renting a garage to store the mattresses in, and he claimed the place was broken into and someone stole his inventory. He made an insurance claim, but then an investigator found out Reuben did it himself."

"He stole his own stuff?"

"Yeah. He took it all to his brother's basement."

"So my mattresses aren't hot?"

"No, no, no." Eric was shocked. "I'd never have put you in touch with him if he was a thief."

"Well, technically, he is," I pointed out. "He's trying to steal from the insurance company, isn't he?"

"Technically, yeah, but see, he had water damage on a pile of beds a year back, and they wouldn't pay. So he was really trying to get straight with them. He's not a thief."

Sometimes Eric's logic escapes me, and I knew better than to dig any deeper. Moving on, I said, "I have some chapters of a book here Reuben wrote and wanted me to look over. I need to get them back to him." I said, rather hopefully, "Is he in prison?"

I'd always wanted to visit someone in prison.

"No, no, he's out on bail. But his wife left him. He's staying with Dumpster Dan. I'll come by after work and pick up his stuff. Is it any good? He's pretty depressed. It would cheer him up if you thought it was any good. He's told everybody you were looking at his work and you told him he was going to have a bestseller. Maybe you could show it to your editor for him; that would really give him a boost."

Lordy. I'd written that dedication never dreaming Reuben would take it seriously, or confuse it with any critique.

"Bobby?" Eric hated dead air time.

I mumbled, "It needs work." Now I'd have to rewrite the critique so the guy didn't head for the bridge when he read it. All I needed was Reuben committing suicide because of something I said.

Writing *anything* is so difficult. No matter how awful the product was, at least Reuben tried. It took me another two hours to reword what I'd said so it sounded vaguely encouraging but not too hopeful. I thought longingly of the new bed I'd been coveting and I called Eric again.

"I guess Reuben can't sell me another mattress set, eh?"

"Nope. They confiscated his inventory. But I know this other guy—"

"Thanks, but I think I'll take a drive over to Beds and

Beyond."

Eric was horrified at the idea that I'd pay full price, but I'd learned another little lesson here: Sometimes full price is by far the most economical way to go.

TIPS ON WRITING

The only worthwhile suggestion I have applies to both writing and running a B&B. It's written on my desk in black indelible ink:

OKAY, UNIVERSE.
YOU DO QUALITY, I'LL DO QUANTITY.

BEAUTIFUL KATIE

I asked for strength, and God gave me difficulties to make me strong.
(Hazrat Inayat Khan, Sufi master)

There's always the question of what to charge when you run a bed and breakfast. Generally, people expect to pay less for more than they'd get at a hotel, and I have no idea why. I charged by the room, which meant one person paid the same as two friendly people. Given my romantic track record, I figured anyone in a reasonable workable relationship deserved a break.

I didn't advertise my rates, and as time went on, I found myself adjusting the nightly fee in accordance with how I felt. If I was exhausted and wanted a night off, I'd double it when someone inquired. Or if a young couple came along with an old car, a baby, and appointments at Children's Hospital, I'd cut it in half.

So when a social worker called asking what my rates were, I asked her why she was inquiring before I quoted. She explained she had a woman from Germany in town visiting her mother in a rest home. The lady was currently staying in a most unsatisfactory B&B, paying much more than she could afford.

The logical questions to me were, "What can she afford? And how long is she staying?"

A figure was quoted. The visit would last four weeks. I

thought it over quickly, cut $10 a day from the amount the social worker had suggested, and waited for my new guest to arrive.

Katie was small and shy and tense, a faded, pretty woman in her late forties, obviously upset. The place she'd been staying had a bully for a landlady. I showed her to her room under the eaves and invited her down for tea whenever she was settled.

"It is very kind of you," she stated, her hands shaking so that tea spilled over the side of the cup. It took a couple of days before she'd calmed down enough to be able to explain what she was doing in Canada.

Late in life, her mother had married a Canadian and come to live here in Vancouver. The gentleman died, and Katie's mom began to exhibit signs of Alzheimer's.

"I am divorced, I live on small pension in a little town in Germany," she explained in her careful, stilted English. "Here, my mother has free medical care. If I bring her back to Germany, I could not afford the care she needs. I would have to care for her myself at home, and I cannot."

"Of course not," I assured her. "My second husband had Parkinson's disease. He wouldn't hear of having anyone else help him but me, and if I hadn't divorced him, I felt I would have died. I shouldn't have stayed as long as I did. Taking responsibility for someone else's problems is not only arrogant, but self defeating for both of you."

She shot me a grateful look. "My life, it has not been happy, or my mother's life, either. And I worry that without family here to visit her, she will not be well treated. The rest home is government, not private. So every year, I save my money and fly to visit her, although she knows me no longer."

Ingenuously, she told me how much her pension was, and I could only imagine the small and large sacrifices she must have to make to afford plane fare and lodging.

"My mother died two years ago," I told her. "I know how difficult it is to see your mother slipping away."

"She lived in Vancouver, your mother?"

I shook my head. "In a little coal mining town about a twelve hour drive from here, in interior British Columbia. The town where I was born, where my brother and sister still live, and most of my nieces and nephews and cousins. I was the only one who moved away from there."

"I think you are very brave, Bobby."

"I didn't feel that way during the time my mother was alive. I felt like a coward much of the time. As the eldest daughter, I was nominated to do the difficult things when I went home for a visit, like telling her she would have to give up her driver's license, move into a senior's home. And I would tremble, telling her. My mother was not an easygoing lady. She had this way of looking at me that made me feel like a child who'd misbehaved."

"Ahhh, I understand. We were not always—how do you say, companionable? My mother and I."

"Compatible. My mother and I weren't either. She was difficult, my mother."

"And mine. I think all mothers are so, no?"

I grinned. "Except for thee and me."

But Katie had no children. She'd been married twice, same as me, and both had ended in divorce. We nibbled cookies, traded war stories, and agreed we weren't going to try again at the marriage sweepstakes.

Katie was the ideal house guest. Quiet and retiring, she kept both her room and the upstairs bathroom pristine. She was gone early each day, spending her time at the hospital. She came home in the evening, drawn and tired. I frequently invited her to share a meal with me, but she never would. She insisted she'd eaten with her mother at the hospital. I guessed she didn't want to feel indebted. Or maybe it was just too stressful, having to speak English and eat at the same time.

She adored my back garden, however, and would spend quiet hours sitting on a lawn chair by the pond, reading. But of course,

Louie interrupted her at regular intervals with tales of Sammy's prowess and rights of ownership to my garden. I'd warned her about him and suggested she might not want to go over and see his house. Early on, I'd been lured into a tour, ostensibly to see his plants, which ended up in his basement where he began showing me photos of nudes. I'd only lived in the neighbourhood a week at that stage, and it dawned on me that no one knew where the hell I was. I doubted Louie was a murderer, but if he was, my body would probably never be found. Breathing heavily, he flipped the pages of the book, and I could see they were art studies instead of hard core porn, but still. There were plenty of boobs and pubic hair on display.

"That's not appropriate," I barked in a trembling voice, edging towards the stairs and the door to freedom. I never ventured into his house again.

Katie clucked her tongue when I told her that. She was coolly polite to Louie, but I could see he irritated her more and more as the days went by, and finally, she couldn't hold it in any longer. She exploded in my kitchen one evening, in a quiet, reasonable, Katie fashion, of course.

Why was Louie allowed to roam around the neighbourhood, disturbing everyone, she asked me? Why was he not in a government home with other people like himself? In Germany, it would be taken care of. Why did I allow him free run of my garden, how could I be so eternally patient with him? Why didn't I tell his guardian, Caroline, once and for all that he was not to be in my back garden all the time? I could put a lock on the garden gate. I could forbid him to trespass on my property. He was—she paused, searching for an English word—he was a disturbance.

I agreed. Louie was indeed a disturbance, a major one. So then I told her the story of my son, David. Dave was born profoundly deaf, and when he was little, wearing his hearing aids and making the loud discordant sounds the deaf often make, well-meaning people often told me I should put him in a home.

"He is in a home," I'd respond, wanting to hit them, wanting to scream, *He's in my home. I'm his mother. Can't you see how much you're hurting me when you say this about my baby, my beloved son?*

Dave was now in his early forties, a skilled carpenter and handyman, married to a woman who was also profoundly deaf. He has two beautiful daughters, both of whom are hearing. He's a fantastic father, a reasonably happy, functional man who has somehow learned to survive quite well in a hearing world. But how was I to know, all those years ago, that things would turn out almost okay? A piece of me had been wounded by deafness, was wounded anew every single day once I knew the name of the calamity that had befallen my child.

"He's not mentally challenged, like Louie is," I told Katie. "But Dave *is* handicapped. And like all handicapped people, life has been tough for him. He was bullied and teased as a child. I remember, when he was about seven, a group of boys chased him and put lit firecrackers down his jacket. They figured he couldn't tell anyone. He had a hard time in school because he was dyslexic as well as deaf. Although he's immensely capable, there are a great number of jobs he can't apply for because they require hearing or reading skills. He's just—different. He talks and lip reads, but some people avoid him because they're afraid they won't be able to understand him."

Katie was listening, looking at me with the expression I'd come to recognize when I told someone about David. It was a combination of pity, compassion, and a sort of shamefaced relief—this was a situation they didn't have to deal with. It was like I had cancer and they didn't. They never knew what to say.

I'd planned to stop there, just leave it as it was, but I suddenly got the bus syndrome. You know, you sit down beside a stranger for a long journey and after a few hours, you pour out stuff you'd never tell the people who think they know you.

"I found out he was deaf when he was fourteen months

old," I said, remembering the medicinal smell of the doctor's white coat, the rank odour on his breath from the cigarette he'd smoked before he came into the stuffy little room where I sat clutching my baby son on my lap. I clearly remember how my knees shook underneath David's diapered bottom, how my belly gurgled because I hadn't been able to eat since I sat in that soundproof cubicle and smiled at my son as noises that hurt my ears didn't make him blink or turn.

"Your baby is profoundly deaf," he'd told me in a detached voice. I started to cry, because I knew it was forever. David wouldn't get over it, not like a cold. And neither would I.

"You can cry for the rest of your life, but it won't help your son," the doctor warned me in a tired voice. "He needs someone to teach him language."

So I took my baby home and did my best. Isn't that what everyone does, the best they know how at the time? That had been forty odd years ago. I smiled at Katie, but I couldn't seem to stop talking.

"David was the most engaging, good-natured baby, smiling at everyone, mimicking facial expressions and actions. He had a perfectly square little face and a wild crop of thick brown hair that grew straight forward, and his eyes were different colours— one blue, one brown. He was my middle child. I was twenty-one when he was born. I'd married at eighteen and had my first, perfect son, ten months later. My husband drank and I was beginning to realize that his abject apologies and promises that he'd never hit me again were not to be believed. For a long time, I thought David was deaf because his father knocked me down and kicked me in the stomach when I was five months pregnant."

It had taken me a long time to forgive not only the man, but the person I'd been then. "I was such a dumb girl," I told Katie. "Until Dave was diagnosed, I didn't even know that babies could be deaf. I thought deafness was something that only happened to old people." I also thought alcoholism was curable, and promises were promises. I did know the earth was round, but that was about the extent of my worldly knowledge.

Katie reached across and laid her slender hand on my big one. Pat pat, pat pat.

"I am sorry this happened to you, Bobby."

"Thank you, but you see, the deafness turned out to be a gift," I said correcting her. "I was an impatient person and it taught me patience. I was proud, and it taught me humility." It also forced me to begin searching for a spiritual path that made sense to me, but I didn't tell Katie that. Time enough in the rest of her four weeks here for me to burst out with my spiritual Tourette's.

"Louie," she said after a long silence. "He also was born this way?"

"I heard it was a shortage of oxygen at birth, but I don't know for sure." I also knew it didn't matter. David's deafness had been studied by geneticists, given a fancy label, documented in something called the Green Journal. All that medical notoriety didn't make him any less deaf.

"Louie's mother lived to a hundred and two, she died five years before I bought this house," I confided. "Louie was an only child, born late in her life. The father died when Louie was young, so there was only him and his mother. She wasn't always kind to him. Caroline says she made him wash all the walls of the house over and over, until even the plaster was ruined. But she also told Caroline she couldn't die until she was sure he'd be cared for, safe in the house where he'd grown up. So Caroline agreed to be his guardian, and Louie's gone on living next door." I grinned at her. "More or less. Whenever he's not roaming in my garden."

Katie didn't smile. "I understand. I thank you for explaining."

"It's just that I know exactly how it was for them. For Louie and his mother. Especially for his mother."

"I hope you will forgive me for what I said."

I put my arms around her and hugged her stiff, slight body. "No forgiveness is necessary, because no sin was committed. No sin ever is."

My belief system embraces the concept that there's only one of us here. Everything outside of me is a projection of myself, of some emotion or action that I really don't want to admit is in me, something I need to look at, acknowledge, forgive. Projection is perception. As I see you, I see myself. As I condemn you, I condemn myself. So the only logical course of action, because I also believe that all of this is a dream, has to be forgiveness for whatever *hasn't* been done. It couldn't have been, because this is a dream, right? When we awaken from a dream, it fades away, it isn't real. All I needed to do was concentrate on loving whatever was in front of me—at this moment, Katie.

"Will you have some homemade soup and bread with me?" I knew she'd say no, she always did, but I went on asking anyway.

Her rare smile flashed, and she was momentarily illuminated. "Thank you, yes. I would very much enjoy."

After that, we had dinner together often.

When Katie's visit came to an end, she asked if she might have a copy of a picture I had on my wall. It was taken at Easter when I was a year and a half old. My mother's hobby was photography, and she'd posed me sitting outside in a little chair, wearing a smart bonnet and matching coat. My fat sausage legs stick straight out in front of me. They're encased in white stockings, my feet in black boots. I'm staring seriously down at a single egg in a bowl on my lap. The photo is black and white. I look pretty much like a dork, a fat Buddha baby studying its navel. Regardless, I had a copy made of the photo and gave it Katie, totally baffled as to why she'd want it. We both cried when she left.

Months later, I received a letter from her with several hundred euros tucked inside, along with a photo of a wall in her house. She'd put my picture at the top of a grouping of family photos. Next to me was Katie when she was little, wrapped in a tiny fur coat, scowling out at the world. On that wall in that house in Germany, we are sisters.

I think the lesson here is that we never know what anything is for. In telling Katie about David, I clarified for myself the mixed feelings I have about Louie. What I do know for sure is that it's never about money.

Every year since then, Katie has sent me a Christmas card with a lovely letter and a hundred euros. I send them back to her, telling her to put the money in a special fund so she can come and stay with me again. But her mother's dead now, and Katie isn't well. It's unlikely she'll ever come back to Canada, and I don't like to travel. So I doubt I shall ever go to Germany.

It doesn't matter. We had our time together.

I'm convinced the guests who come to the Blue Collar have a contract with me, made long ago. We have things between us to settle, to forgive, to understand. I don't know what those things are, or why they're important. I only know that those who are meant to come to you will come. Your job as host is simply to offer a comfortable pillow top bed, a lavish breakfast, an attentive, listening ear, and as much non-judgment and forgiveness as you can muster up on any given day.

Sometimes—rarely, and only when it's relevant—you can offer snippets of your so-called life. But keep it brief and topical. Keep in mind people don't want to listen. They're often desperate to be heard. Listening is your job. It should also be your pleasure.

Blue Collar B & B

SPIRITUAL TOURETTE'S
(Or another version of the Big Bang theory)

(I'm nowhere near smart enough to have figured this out on my own. There's a great book called The End of Reincarnation *by Gary Renard that explains it much better than this.)*

Before the beginning, all was joyous extension. No beginnings and endings, only eternity. Created in the Creator's image, we were unflawed oneness, existing in boundless, unimaginable ecstasy. What happened next didn't really happen at all. As in a dream, it only appeared to occur to one small aspect of the Whole. It was a tiny, mad idea, something like, what would it be like if I went off and played by myself?

The Creator didn't respond to it because the idea was not of perfect oneness. And what is not perfect oneness cannot exist in the Creator's eternity. But in that cosmic instant of seeming separation, we fell asleep, and in our dreams duality was born, and the ego.

Deep inside, we have the memory of perfect oneness, calling us to return, to waken from the dream, but one thing led to another, and waking up became more and more difficult for us as we created time and projection and individuality, which seemed to produce more and more aspects of ourselves.

Because with that tiny, mad idea, fear was also born, the horrific feeling that we'd done something terribly wrong arose in us. Separating was monumental and we would be punished for it. And so the ego rose to the occasion, saying, "You're in big trouble now. You've pissed off the Creator, and It's going to get you for this. But I know a place the Creator isn't even aware of. You can hide there, you'll be safe there." Other, wiser voices said, Don't be silly. There is no such thing as punishment. You know you are Love, pure and simple.

But our fear was overwhelming, and everything was strange and topsy-turvy, so we agreed to side with the ego and in that instant, this universe was created. That was the Big Bang, and we made earth and stars and animals and guilt and sin and all that we mistakenly label reality.

And thus we became enmeshed in density, in duality, in this pesky dream of separation, and in this entire imaginary creation of ours, this universe, which has absolutely nothing to do with our Creator. It—He, She, All That Is—isn't even aware of the existence of this crazy place. How could It be when It is perfect Love? As for us, we are not really here at all. We're safe at Home, but we're having trouble waking up.

The events in a dream are of no consequence because they're not really happening. Knowing that doesn't make it any easier for us to endure the seemingly endless lifetimes we spend here, or the pain we inflict on ourselves because we feel we deserve it and more for that first mistake, because the events in this dream feel real to us, and the wheel of reincarnation is not easy to get off. It has been done, by Jesus, and Buddha, and Krishnamurti, and countless others, all of whom illustrated that it can be done by you and I, by the application of true forgiveness—by totally accepting that you haven't done anything to me at all, or I to you. How could we hurt one another if this is a dream, and you, my beloved, are just another extension of myself? You are giving me a gift by allowing me to choose forgiveness—Love—instead of blame.

Every single thing that appears to happen to us is really an opportunity, another chance to change, not the world, but the way we view the world. My choice is to see you as myself.

This is my belief system and it works for me. The only true test of any spiritual concept is whether or not it brings joy and peace and comfort when we find our baby is deaf, or our mother is dying. I'd never presume to say this is right for you. For me, it keeps me on the straight and narrow. It gives me direction.

I'm trying to apply it. I've been trying on an hourly basis for maybe twenty years. Most days I make it to noon without judging. I'd like to think I'm getting better at it, but I'm reminded pretty often of how far there is still to go. And reminded, as well, that angels fly because they take themselves lightly.

SECOND TO THE RIGHT, AND THEN STRAIGHT ON TILL MORNING

(Peter Pan, by J.M. Barrie)

"Bobby. It's me."

The warm, sexy male voice on the phone belonged to Steve, whom I'd labelled Peter Pan. He loved the nickname. He didn't know about the line in the movie that said about Peter, *He cannot love, its part of his condition.* Or the line in Barrie's magical book that described Peter as *innocent and heartless.*

I'd met Steve six months before I opened the Blue Collar. I was walking along the river early one morning and a tall, muscular gorgeous man fell into step beside me. He was a Phys Ed teacher at a local school who had a window cleaning business on the side.

Steve had a slight stammer which I found endearing, along with his wide smile and an air of total attentiveness. He'd never been married, he currently lived with his mother who needed his assistance, but he said he hoped to be able to move into an apartment of his own soon again. We found out that we worked out at the same gym, although I hadn't seen him there.

He was younger than me by twelve years, which I pointed out near the end of our walk. I'd been told that in spite of my crop of snow-white hair, I didn't look my age, and Steve repeated that compliment several times. Really, how much difference is there between 60 and 48? Not enough to matter, apparently, because he asked for my phone number, and I hadn't been home half an hour before he called and asked if I wanted to go for a ride that evening.

An intelligent younger man. A date. How exciting. Of course I wanted to go for a ride.

He drove up in a very old powder blue Cadillac. He liked old cars, he told me. This one wasn't vintage; it was just old and battered with bench seat, cracked leather upholstery, set seat belts that wouldn't always fasten, windows that didn't close or didn't open. It didn't matter, it was summer in Vancouver. There was a huge yellow moon hanging out over the water, and the downtown city was humming like a tuning fork.

Steve had once owned a music store, and he had tapes from all the rock and roll bands. He played Tom Petty, Elvis, Rod Stewart, Neil Young, Barry White as he drove me around the city, showing me awnings he'd cleaned, views from obscure hilltops, the house where he'd grown up. We had pizza at an obscure little place at the foot of Main Street. I felt myself growing younger by the moment.

Steve didn't drink or smoke. He attended a Pentecostal church every Sunday morning. I couldn't help but notice he was rather obsessive. He closed the car door three times whenever he got out or in. He did the same with the door at the café. He genuflected, one knee on the floor, before he sat down in the booth. His belief system was rigid—he was more than a little homophobic, critical of anyone he considered overweight, and not sympathetic to anyone of colour.

Highly controlling, I deduced. Maybe the child of alcoholic parents? I asked, and he denied it, although I later found out I was right. But hey, who among us is without foibles? I wasn't planning to marry him. I'd obviously drawn him into my life to teach me something. And there was no one else on the horizon at the moment, always a good argument for overlooking someone's wounds.

When he asked me out again, this time on a Friday night, I went gladly. I found him weirdly attractive, and yes, I was flattered that he seemed to feel the same about me. This time he said, "I have to pick up two friends of mine, Eric and Roger. We always spend Friday night together. Roger's a pain in the ass, but you'll like Eric. He's the smartest guy I ever met. We grew up on the same block."

He drove down an alley and honked the horn and a young Oriental man trotted out and climbed into the back seat.

"Bobby, this is Eric," Steve said. And that's how I met the guy who became my dearest friend.

We drove around the block and down the street, stopped again, honked the horn, and Roger came out, a pudgy man with a whiney voice, unhealthy colour, and what seemed a really bad attitude. He got in the back beside Eric.

By the end of that first evening, I agreed with Steve. Roger was irascible. Eric was brilliant. He was also more than a little peculiar—but they all were, which I found fascinating. Unlike the other two, Eric had been married and divorced twice, like me.

I suspected that Roger was gay, and when he came out to his friends a few months later, Steve was devastated, furious, and betrayed. He insisted he'd had no idea. Of course, Eric knew.

Eric worked in a back room as an underpaid dental mechanic, although he'd passed the real estate board exam and could probably have been a nuclear scientist or a brain surgeon. He had a mind that trapped chunks of information about millions of different subjects and regurgitated them at will. He was a walking research department for a writer. He was curious about everything, open to any weird hypothesis, made friends of the most unlikely people, and had a childlike eagerness about the world. He was consistently good natured, read indiscriminately, as I did, and he loved words for their own sake. And he could repair anything.

Like Steve, both Eric and Roger still lived at home. Roger worked for Steve at the window cleaning business, and while Eric and I talked about transcendental meditation and The Dancing Wu Lei Masters, they bickered about the safety of ladders, the best time to start in the morning, the manner in which customers should be treated, and what tape to play next.

That first Friday was the beginning of my strange midlife summer spent driving around in cars with three men I labelled the Lost Boys. They were all chronologically middle aged, although emotionally they'd never really grown up. They didn't want to. When I asked what they wanted out of life, Steve answered for all of them by misquoting Cindy Lauper: "Boys just want to have fun."

None of them travelled outside the Lower Mainland—unlike the real Peter Pan, they were all afraid of flying. None of them was currently involved in any sort of committed relationship. None owned real estate. Roger and Eric didn't own or drive cars.

None lived independently. Steve, I found out, had only lived on his own once—for two weeks, at which point he hightailed it back home to Mom.

Eric used his bike for transportation and wore his bike helmet like a security blanket. He spent every Sunday morning making lunch for his mother and father. None of them drank, or smoked, or—as far as I could tell—fornicated much, if at all.

Despite his studly appearance and seductive attentiveness, Steve and I made love exactly once, about two weeks after I'd met him. It seemed to go well, at least as well as first encounters ever do. I looked forward to a repeat performance, but although he went on calling me every evening, taking me to the gym, inviting me on long walks or to the beach, and of course picking me up for those Friday night expeditions, Steve never again laid a hand or lip or other body part on me. I was baffled and hurt. Not to brag, but my prowess as a sensual, desirable woman had never before been called into question. Until now, no one had ever kicked me out of bed, literally or figuratively.

I talked The Situation over with my women friends, all of whom were as mystified as I was. None of us had come across this particular version of male battiness.

I finally asked him point-blank what had turned him off sexually with me, and he said that it wasn't me at all. Because of his religion, he was saving himself for marriage, and he'd never met a woman who qualified to be his wife. I, sadly, didn't qualify because I was too old.

Stunned, I thought that one over. Had my vagina shrivelled up when I was paying too much attention to my fingernails, I demanded? Or was it simply that I was post-menopausal and couldn't produce an heir and a spare? Oh no, he assured me. He wasn't planning on having children—he saw enough of them in school and didn't want the responsibility. No, it was just that he preferred younger women. They were less opinionated.

I'm afraid I laughed until I couldn't stand up, and he took umbrage and didn't call me again for two weeks. But then he did, as if nothing had ever happened, and I climbed back into the old Caddie because I missed Eric and the music and those addictive hot summer nights that made me feel sixteen again. (How much older than Peter was Wendy, anyhow?)

Steve was always careful to drop me off last on Fridays. I suspected he wanted his friends to believe he and I were having a torrid affair, the sad, bad, crazy man. What was really going on was that with a little encouragement, (writers are notoriously curious, I have to know what's going on at the back of everyone's head) Steve began to confide in me about other women he'd dated, and I realized that he went about every conquest the same way—charming the woman out of her panties, exactly once, and then driving the poor lady berserk by suddenly becoming celibate. It was the strangest case of coitus interruptus I'd ever come across, and of course it had everything to do with an extreme need to control and nothing whatsoever to do with religion or age or wifely qualifications.

As time went on, he became more and more open with me about his conquests, even bringing a couple of them over to meet me, exhibiting a trust that boggled the mind.

(Actually, one of my former husbands did the same thing. He brought a lady friend home to meet me. She asked why we'd divorced, and when I told her physical and mental cruelty, she dumped him. Go figure.)

Steve had always phoned me a number of times each day—part of his obsessive nature—and now he began phoning late every evening, after *The Soprano's* finished. He loved the show and would dump us all off early so he could get home in time to watch it. He'd talk far into the night about dating teachers, waitresses, hairdressers, artists—even a rather well-known country western star. You name the category, Steve had sampled it—according to Steve. I had my doubts. I finally asked Eric if even half of his stories were true, and Eric said he was pretty much telling the truth; he'd witnessed the hit parade. Not the sex part, but the women, and the slow, seductive build-up followed by the quick reversal. Apparently, Steve paraded his females in front of his friends like trophies, which of course they were. He was Da Man. And the man was a walking flytrap when it came to women. He should have come with a warning label.

The summer turned to fall. I started the B&B and became too busy to play with the lost boys on Friday evenings. Steve found yet another unsuspecting female to focus his attention on and after I got call display and stopped taking his calls, he stopped phoning me. Roger came out of the closet and began to hang around with gay friends, bringing them over to meet me, which I very much enjoyed. They were, frankly, mostly weird, scary smart, and so wickedly sarcastic I couldn't help but adore them.

They asked me to their parties, insisting that with a little help in the wardrobe department and some hair colour, I could double for Cher, which was patently untrue, but immensely flattering.

Eric took to dropping by for tea and conversation—with his tool box. I hadn't seen or heard from Steve for months when the phone call came.

"It's Peter Pan. How's it going?"

We exchanged pleasantries before he said, "Do you have room for a guest this coming week? She's flying in from Brunei." His deep, seductive voice oozed repressed excitement. "She works for the Sultan. We met on the Internet and she's coming to meet me. Her name's Jane."

Jane, who worked for the Sultan of Brunei, flying all the way to Vancouver to meet Steve? Even for him, this was a stretch. Intrigued, I checked my calendar and reserved a room, already feeling sorry for Jane, who couldn't have the slightest idea what she was getting into.

Steve was beside himself. In his entire career as a one-night-stand lothario, no woman had ever flown across half the world to be with him. It was whipped cream on his sundae.

He began phoning me again every day, drunk with the romance and excitement of it all, speculating about whether or not she'd been part of the Sultan's harem and how rich she was—everyone in Brunei was rich, the Sultan was the richest man in the world, things equal to the same thing, etc.

In between Steve's obsessive phone calls I did some research on Brunei, a tiny country on the northwest border of Borneo. His Majesty Sultan Haji Hassanal Bolkiah Muzzaddin Waddaulah was the Supreme Ruler, and until recently he *was* one of the richest men in the world, thanks to Shell Oil. Oil is his country's only resource, but fortunately, supply seems unlimited. His fortune was estimated at 40 billion, but unfortunately, he's now down to a mere 10 big ones—peanuts when it comes to international wealth these days.

Blue Collar B & B

So how did he blow 30 billion? A bit of research put it down to plain old financial incompetence, way too much fun, and perhaps the prolonged fall in the price of oil and the Asian crash of 1997. The Sultan, it goes without saying, is a big spender who likes to have a good time. He built a palace with 1,788 rooms, probably because he could. Among other toys, he has 2000 luxury limos—in a country sadly lacking in roads—plus his own jumbo jet which normally seats 400. Oh, and he has six smaller planes and two helicopters as well.

He and his brother built Jerudong Park, a theme park like Disneyland, which cost a cool billion. It used to be free for the citizens of Brunei, but due to the Sultan's financial difficulties, there's now a nominal entrance fee. But forget the harem. The Sultan only has two wives. He's allowed to have four at any given moment, but he's a man who shows great restraint in certain areas, obviously. Or else the high cost of Viagra has curtailed him. He has only eleven children.

He divorced one wife, a former flight attendant, instead of just demoting her to third place. It wasn't an amicable divorce. He stripped the poor woman of all her royal titles before he replaced her with a TV star, 32 years his junior. It's a wonder he didn't have his last duchess beheaded, because he could.

His subjects are not allowed to vote. He is the Sultan by birth, but by his own decree he is also the Prime Minister, the Minister of Defense and the Minister of Finance. In 2006, he reportedly changed Brunei's constitution to make himself infallible under Bruneian law.

Obviously, a self-made man.

To give the guy his due, he has made an effort to share some of his wealth with his subjects. Brunei is known as the Shellfare State. No one pays personal or corporation taxes, medical services are free, as is education. Clearly, his subjects aren't rolling in green if Jane was staying with me instead of booking into the Pan Pacific down on the waterfront. Steve had overlooked the fact that the Blue Collar offers exceptional value for the money, but a five-star resort it ain't.

J Day finally arrived. I was watching from the front window when Steve drove up. He'd washed the Caddie. He was wearing a dark suit and he looked exceptionally handsome. He also looked exceptionally downcast. As he helped Jane out and shouldered her luggage, I could see that all was not well. Knowing Steve, it wasn't hard for me to figure out what some of the problems were even before they came in the house.

Jane was very dark skinned, a fact I later learned had somehow escaped his notice on the Internet. She was also more than a little plump, and given his list of prejudices, those two items alone were enough to turn him off.

She, on the other hand, was glowing. She was cradling the bouquet of flowers I'd suggested he take to the airport to welcome her, and judging by her lovesick expression whenever she glanced his way, she was down for the count.

Steve introduced us, avoiding my gaze, and said he was sorry but he had to go, he was in the middle of a window washing job, which I knew to be a lie. He'd told me he was taking the day off to show her around. The rat was skittering off the tilting ship. But Jane surprised us both by reminding him in a firm, loud voice that he was showing her around Vancouver and then taking her out to dinner, yes? She had to freshen up, it had been a long flight, but then she expected him to come by for her. Exactly what time was he picking her up? And, oh yes, she wanted to meet the voice teacher he'd said he knew, she wanted some lessons while she was here. And had he managed to get her the special rate he'd promised?

Steve mumbled that he'd see about it.

"Please do so right away, because I am here for only a week this first time," Jane said in an imperious tone. "There is no time to waste."

Steve blanched at this reference to subsequent visits.

"Now," she said. "What time shall I expect you?"

"Five," Steve mumbled. It was Friday and I figured he'd be picking up Eric at seven. He was rigid about his Friday routine. He'd probably corral Roger as well, gay or not. My hunch was he'd take refuge in numbers so as not to be alone with Jane.

He made his escape, looking hunted.

A WORD FROM MY MOTHER TO THE SULTAN

You never see a U-Haul hitched behind a hearse.

KARMA RULES

I took Jane up to her room, invited her for tea, and when she came down, I settled back to hear her side of Steve and the Brunei romance.

"Steven and I met on an Internet dating site three months ago," she gushed in her accented lilting English. "I, too, am a teacher and also a student of music, so we have much in common."

A teacher? Steve had insinuated she was at least the Sultan's personal secretary.

"You teach the Sultan's children?"

She looked at me as if I was mentally challenged.

"No, no, no, of course not, there are special governesses who do that. I have nothing to do with the Sultan whatsoever. His children are dreadfully spoiled, they get everything they want. No, no, no. I teach in the general school system. We have very good schools in Brunei, although the students are not well-behaved. They lack discipline. In my family, discipline was important."

So much for Steve's bragging. But when I thought it over, of course technically Jane did work for the Sultan. From what I'd learned about the place, everybody in Brunei worked for the Sultan because he's the big kahuna who owns and runs everything. And everyone, when it comes down to it.

"You sing?" I recalled the bit about the teacher of voice.

"Oh, yes." She puffed up like a rooster ruffling its feathers.

"I have studied voice for many, many, many years. I sing in the church choir, and I have a recital when I go home, which is why I need to meet this very good voice teacher Steven knows."

I made appreciative, noncommittal noises. Another of Steve's foibles was passing well-known people off as his personal friends when all he'd done was wash their windows. But Jane was again waxing poetic about dear Steven.

"Both of us 35, both single, both lonely."

Lonely? I doubted Steve had spent a lonely day in his adult life. He was terrified of being alone. Whenever he wasn't with his posse or his latest conquest, he was on the phone to me. And 35? I knew for a fact that Steve was now 51, and that he'd taken out at least six other women (that I knew about) during that three month period, but I have a rule that I try to live by: there are only three kinds of business in this world. There's my business, your business and God's business. I have no business in two of those, even though I like to hear about them. I can listen, nod, express compassion, ask questions, but I'm not allowed to meddle. I'm certainly not supposed to judge.

But omigod, it's such a challenge. I bit my tongue and tried not to choke on my tea as she went on about finally meeting a man with the same religious convictions she had, a man of high moral standards, who, like her, had enough self control to wait for marriage before having sexual relations. Gasp!

I said, "Is there a shortage of available men in Brunei?"

She made a disparaging motion with her hand.

"There are men enough, but they are interested in only one thing: sex, sex, sex." She spat the word out as if it tasted bad. "There is no respect for a woman with principles, you see, not at all. Many, many, many men have courted me, but when I insisted on remaining chaste, they showed their true colours."

"Ahhhh, I see." Steve and a 35-year-old determined virgin. It was going to be an interesting week.

I soon learned that Jane wanted what she wanted when she

wanted it. She ordered breakfast for precisely 8:15 a.m.—melon and whole wheat toast, lightly buttered, plain yogurt and café au lait. It was all simple enough to prepare, but that didn't mean I got to sleep in.

The first morning of her stay and every morning thereafter, the entire neighbourhood and I were yanked from slumber at 5:15. She insisted on practicing operatic scales at the top of her considerable lungs with the upstairs window wide open.

That performance took her until 7:30 to complete. I'm not tone deaf, but neither am I an expert on voice. She sounded loud and shrill to me, but hey, what did I know? Besides the fact that someone was certain to complain if this kept up, particularly because Sammy took it upon himself to sit below her window and join in. Between Jane and the damned cat, only someone as profoundly deaf as David could have slept.

I suggested she close the windows. She insisted she needed fresh air if her vocal chords were to open in the proper manner. And could I please serve her guava juice instead of orange, which was much, much, much too acidic for her throat. And did I have a small space heater? It was colder here than she was used to. And, please, another blanket on the bed, not wool, she was highly allergic to wool; she preferred a goose down duvet. With a cotton cover. Oh, and the pillow, it was feathers, yes? She didn't like feather pillows. She needed a soft synthetic pillow, if I didn't mind. Three, actually. She always slept with one between her knees, which might have explained how and why she'd remained a virgin all these years.

That first morning, she used my phone to try and track Steve down. He'd unwisely given her numbers for both his cell and his home. Obviously caught off guard, he answered her call and she bullied him into taking her to Granville Island Market, and then to meet the voice coach, and then to the gardens at Little Mountain, a breathtakingly beautiful man-made park on the top of a mountain in the heart of Vancouver.

As the week progressed, Steve stopped answering his phones. Her recorded messages to him became increasingly strident and accusatory. She'd walk around my living room as she talked to his machines, banging her feet down, face purple with indignation. She progressed to ever more furious messages, delivered in her loud voice. She'd slam down the receiver, demanding of me, "Why did he bring me this long distance only to avoid me? Not that he paid my fare, oh no, no, no, he is far too cheap for that, am I right? Not once does he take me to a decent restaurant, only that disgusting pizza place. I am beginning to suspect he is not a man of honour, do you not agree?"

Of course I didn't agree. I knew Steve probably had the first dollar he'd ever earned, but I'd never wanted him to pay for my pizza. Besides, I was having a hard time feeling compassionate towards Jane. She had some new complaint every morning—the toast was cold, the muffins gave her gas, the yogurt wasn't sweet enough, the coffee was too strong. She was a difficult guest. I had to repeatedly ask myself what there was here for me to learn. It soon became evident that patience was the issue for me, because she tried mine in every possible way.

By the fourth day, Steve was calling me at all hours, insisting she was stalking him. He'd unwisely mentioned a window washing job he had on Granville Street, and she took a bus there and found him, and then proceeded to give advice for the next two hours on how he could best do his job. She'd even taken a taxi to his mother's house, horror of all horrors.

I knew from Eric that Steve never introduced any of his women to his mother. Jane simply looked up his address in the phone book, took the bus over, and knocked on the door when he was at work. Apparently, she insinuated to Mother that she and Steve were all but engaged. Steve's mother was incensed because he'd never mentioned this woman, and to top it off she was *coloured*. It seemed Steve had come by his prejudices honestly.

Just as I'd suspected, Steve had taken Eric along with him and Jane on nearly every outing, and now she began calling Eric at work to complain about Steve. So Eric called Steve and told him he'd have to make her cease and desist, as Eric's boss didn't take kindly to fourteen personal calls before noon. Of course, Steve then called me, frantic because Eric was mad at him. He couldn't stand anyone mad at him. Not his men friends or his mother, at any rate. Other women, well, that was a different story. Plenty of them must have become mad enough to castrate him, but his solution was simply to avoid them and move on. Apparently, none of them had shown Jane's perseverance.

Eric called me next, wanting to know what was going on, really. I told him it was more of the same old Steve, but a whole lot more than the gentleman had bargained for.

When Steve phoned again, whining about being stalked, I not-so-gently reminded him that he'd encouraged Jane to come to Canada, and therefore he did have some responsibility towards her while she was here.

"But she's not a nice lady," he wailed in my ear. "She's not suitable."

Big surprise there. Mary Magdalene wouldn't have been suitable either, virgin or no virgin.

"She's driving me crazy. I'm scared to answer my phone. She says she's suing me for breach of promise, but I didn't promise her anything, honest. I've never met anyone like her before. She's using me, treating me like her personal chauffeur, making me drive her all over the city, forcing me to take her out to eat. She even phoned the principal at my school and had him drag me out of class, claiming an emergency."

I believed him. Jane was as persistent as a case of hives, but nevertheless, there were only two days left before he was taking her back to the airport. He *was* taking her back to the airport, right?

Silence. Deep, martyred sighs. Alright, yes, he'd drive her to the airport. He couldn't wait to see the last of her.

The evening before her departure, Jane had a total meltdown in my kitchen. Steve hadn't planned anything special for her last night in Vancouver, she wailed. In fact, he hadn't planned anything at all. She'd phoned him over and over, and he didn't return her calls—not too surprising, considering the blame, anger, dictatorial orders and outright nastiness in the messages she'd been leaving him.

She cried and smashed one of my best tea cups in the sink. She threw a tantrum comparable to any two-year-old's, and I was thankful that there were no other guests in residence. She would sue him for misrepresentation, she shrieked. He'd misled her; she'd believed he was in love with her. She'd spent money on a plane ticket and new clothes and taxis; she wanted full compensation for every single expense. She wasn't a wealthy woman. He was a liar, he was cheap, he was a user of women, he was not going to get away with this—no, no, no.

This money talk didn't make me too comfortable, partly because she hadn't paid me for her week's stay. I'd never had a guest leave without paying, but I had a feeling it was about to happen. I'd noticed that she, too, rubbed every penny twice before spending it. She and Steve had more in common than they realized.

"And you!" she hollered at me. "He says you are his friend. How can you be a friend to someone like him?"

I'd given that a lot of thought. "What is, is. He's doing the best he knows how," I tried to explain. "All of us, at any given moment, are doing the best we know how. If we knew better, we'd do better." And I was at that moment struggling hard to apply this to Jane.

She snorted, gave me a look, and stomped off upstairs. But the next morning, she'd calmed down. She paid me, counting it out to the last penny, and thanked me for her stay.

Steve, true to his word, although more than a little stone-faced, had come to take her to the airport. He was at the curb, waiting with the passenger door open. He'd stowed her luggage in the trunk. He was wearing a brimmed cap. I thought he was overdoing the chauffeur bit just a little.

"Come to Brunei and visit me," Jane said as she walked out the door. "I left my address on the table in my room."

It took me a moment to regain control of my jaw.

"Thank you, Jane. That's very sweet of you." Of course I had no intention of ever doing so—I was about as relieved to see the last of her as Steve was—but I was touched she'd invited me.

She jerked her chin at him. "To think I had dreams of marrying him and moving here. How could I have been so foolish?"

And suddenly I felt terribly sorry for her. I knew about dreams and how much it hurt when they didn't materialize. So I gave her a hug and my best advice about romance and life in general.

She waved as they drove off. I collapsed on the couch, thinking that after all, it was a shame Jane wasn't the Sultan's personal assistant. Things would be a lot better organized in Brunei. Haji Hassanal whatever would have fewer toys and only one wife at a time. His children would be better behaved. He'd probably have his billions intact, earning interest, although there'd be a much higher entrance fee for Jerudong Park. But one thing was certain: the Sultan certainly wouldn't be having quite so much fun—no, no, no.

Just ask Steve.

Blue Collar B & B

BLUE COLLAR ADVICE ON DREAMS AND RELATIONSHIPS

Dreams—and significant others—are like buses. There's always another one coming down the street. And if this one didn't stop for you, it just wasn't your bus. By ranting and raving and flagging it down, you're blocking the way for yours, which is trying to pull up in front of you, but can't because of the obstruction. Let go, smile, and start watching for the next one.

MONEY IS LIKE WATER

One thing the aspiring bed and breakfast host should keep in mind is that this is no way to get rich. Running a B&B will certainly augment your income and you can legitimately deduct a certain percentage of expenses on income tax returns, things like food, bedding, toiletries, and electricity. But your rooms won't be rented a hundred percent of the time. In fact, they might sit empty while you chew your toenails to the quick wondering how to pay this month's Visa bill, which is pretty much why I decided to develop the basement and rent it out on a regular basis. It was already semi-developed, and with Eric's help, several visits to the Goodwill and a few coats of paint, he and I turned it into a modest furnished three bedroom suite, complete with tiny kitchen. I added a second-hand washer and drier and put an ad in the paper.

There were drawbacks, however, and I was anxious about them. There was an electric toilet because the city sewer line came in too high to allow for an ordinary flush type, and anything except body waste and plain toilet paper would ruin the motor.

My electrical panel was in one of the downstairs bedrooms, and each time I blew a fuse upstairs, I'd have to bother whoever was down there to reset the breaker for me. And, as always, there was Louie and Sammy.

My renters would have to be compassionate and patient. It would also help if they liked cats, because Sammy had a habit of sneaking in whenever the basement door was open. And Louie's curiosity knew no boundaries.

The first evening the ad appeared, a sweet-voiced woman asked if she and her husband could come and see the place. Miriam and Tal were a strikingly handsome young couple newly arrived from Israel. They were orthodox Jews. He was a rabbi, wearing a black suit, white shirt and yarmulke. She wore a headscarf covering every bit of her hair, a long-sleeved, plain dress down to her ankles, and sturdy boots, but the frumpy clothing couldn't disguise how beautiful and delicate she was.

They had four adorable children, the oldest a sombre girl of eight, the youngest a cherub of four months. Miriam nursed him while we talked. I told them I wasn't sure about renting to anyone with young children, not because I didn't like kids but because the garden wasn't suitable as a play area. There was a fish pond where a child could drown. I explained about Louie and the cat. I showed them the electrical toilet and went into detail about the dangers of toys or diapers accidentally going south. I showed them the location of the breaker box, and described the inconvenience when I blew a breaker.

Tal assured me the toilet was acceptable, they'd be ultra cautious about unsuitable waste. As for my pond, the children were supervised constantly, he insisted. Miriam didn't work outside the home, and she wouldn't mind resetting the breakers when I blew them. Louie wasn't a problem or Sammy either. Their religion stipulated compassion. They'd be exceptional tenants: quiet, well-behaved, clean.

I sensed they were desperate. They were staying with a friend who had a small house, and the friendship was being strained. Please, would I rent to them? They offered numerous references, all members of the nearby Jewish temple. I had serious reservations. Four small children could mean noisy chaos as well as plugged drains. I had only the fuzziest concepts of traditional orthodox Jewish practices. What would happen if I had Moslem guests? But I looked at Miriam and saw the dark circles under her lovely brown eyes, the strain at the corners of her mouth.

They moved in on Wednesday. On Thursday, Tal took the stove burners outside and purified them and all the kitchen utensils with a blowtorch, narrowly avoiding setting fire to the deck supports. We had to hose them down to stop the smouldering. It was my first faint hint that he wasn't the handiest guy on the planet.

On Friday, I started learning about Shabbat, which apparently meant that from sundown Friday until sundown Saturday things downstairs came to a total standstill. No turning lights on or off—electricity was verboten, which was difficult, considering it was a basement suite, to say nothing of the cursed electric toilet. I'd been worried about this contraption, concerned that it might not stand up to five people using it. I'd never even considered the horror of five people using it and not flushing it for twenty-four hours.

I told Tal something would have to give in that regard, so he prayed over it and finally proclaimed that the second youngest child could flick the switches for the lights and press the flusher on the toilet. She was apparently too young to be affected by whatever the ban on electricity meant. She was too tiny to reach the breaker box, however, and all I could do was hope I didn't blow a fuse Friday evening or Saturday till sundown.

Apparently water usage was also strictly limited on Shabbat. All bathing and laundry had to be accomplished before the sun set on Friday, which meant the hot water supply for the entire house was exhausted by noon. All cooking had to be done ahead of time. The outside light was a problem, because it was on a rheostat and went on automatically. Could I turn it off from Friday evening until Saturday night, Tal asked? It was a security light, so I said a firm no.

They invited me for dinner on Saturday evening. The suite was gleaming clean, the children charming, the food delicious—Miriam must have spent Friday before sundown working her ass off. I noticed that one bedroom, the largest one, contained only a desk and a computer. The kids informed me that this room was daddy's office and they weren't allowed in, so all the children occupied bunks in the medium-sized bedroom, and Miriam and Tal had the smallest space, a tiny bedroom off the kitchen.

While we ate, Tal did most of the talking and Miriam served us and fed the children. He told me they had a house in Jerusalem, but because of the war and the bombing, they'd made the decision to come to Canada. He'd been born in Vancouver, so emigration wasn't an issue. He had dual citizenship.

Miriam was from London. They'd met and married when she went to Jerusalem to work on a kibbutz. Neither had been orthodox Jews until Tal decided to become a rabbi in a very strict sect, some time after their marriage. I asked Miriam what work she'd done before the kids came along.

"I was a fitness instructor," she said. She smiled at my transparent expression. "It was before we became orthodox. I wore shorts and Lycra."

I wondered how it would feel to go from sportswear to total body wrap. I didn't think it represented liberation, but hey, it wasn't up to me to judge.

The first months of their stay in my basement were a learning curve for me regarding Judaic rules and regulations. Tal had no steady job, which was a fortunate thing because observing all the religious holidays took up most of his time. He *was* hooked into some pyramid scheme involving real estate—I attended one of his meetings at his invitation—but judging by how many times the rent was late, it wasn't profitable. He wasn't the best tempered man, either. I could often hear him berating Miriam and the children for something or other.

Shabbat quickly became a major issue. The washing machine broke down—it wasn't up to the eight or ten loads a day Miriam had to do—and Eric wanted to fix it on Saturday. Tal refused him entry because it was Shabbat, so I had to hire a repairman on Monday.

True to form, I regularly blew breakers either late on Friday or Saturday. Tal complained bitterly when I insisted on going down and flicking them back on.

One peculiar religious celebration involved building a hut in my garden out of palm leaves and poles, in which Tal lived for a week. Miriam and the kids brought him his meals, and presumably he used the inside bathroom. But when the week was over, he didn't take the shack down right away as he'd assured me he would. After three weeks, the ramshackle structure was falling apart and Mavis was due to arrive for my monthly gardening session. I set a deadline—it had to be gone by Sunday. Even then, Tal put it off until the last possible moment. He wasn't the most ambitious man around.

But I fell head-over-heels in love with the kids, particularly the second youngest girl, Leah. She was two and a half, a serious, curly-headed angel who took to visiting me in my studio every day. I explained I had to work, and as I wrote, she played quietly with the books and puzzles I found for her at yard sales. I wasn't supposed to give her any snacks except fruit; my kitchen wasn't kosher, but I reasoned that a few chocolate chip cookies couldn't do her that much spiritual harm. She didn't think so either.

It became obvious that Shabbat was synonymous with parental sex. The kids were routinely locked out of the basement every Saturday afternoon. They came upstairs and visited me, the oldest girl—Ruth—toting the baby. Much as I liked them, it didn't make my life any easier.

Inevitably, Miriam was soon once again pregnant. Tal had explained that there were substantial bonuses in Jerusalem for very large families. After a certain number of children—I think he said seven—there was no need for the father to work because the government gave the family enough money to live on.

Obviously, he was aiming for that, and I began to have sleepless nights wondering how many bodies might end up living in my basement. I was beginning to feel like a slum landlord. This would be the fifth pregnancy in eight years for Miriam. It hurt my heart to see her sitting on a bench in my garden, nursing one baby while increasingly pregnant with another. She asked whether I minded if her mother and sister came from England to be with her when the baby was born, and of course I said it was fine, although where they'd sleep in that already overcrowded basement was beyond me.

Miriam brought them to meet me when they arrived, and it was immediately evident that they weren't orthodox. Beautiful women, they both wore makeup, trendy tops and jeans, and had tousled, up-to-the moment haircuts. Miriam's mother was a no nonsense lady with a definite presence, and I could tell she was appalled at the way her daughter was living.

Tal, who usually didn't stir until noon, now took to leaving the house before 7 a.m., looking hunted. He stayed away until at least 5 p.m., which no one seemed to mind.

The baby, another beautiful girl, arrived right on time with no fanfare, and two weeks later, Miriam's family left, also with no fanfare. But the sound of Tal's angry voice could be heard more now, penetrating the floorboards, and Miriam cried as she nursed first the new baby and then the old one in the garden.

I went out to her one day and put an arm around her. "What can I do to help?"

She turned her head into my shoulder and sobbed quietly for a few moments. "I feel like a baby machine," she finally managed. "I'm going home to England with the children before I can get pregnant again. My mother's sending me tickets. We have no money and Tal won't get a steady job. I've told him it's only for a visit, but I won't be back. It's hard to leave him, but I don't know what else to do. I can't live like this anymore. I feel as if I'm dying."

"Then you must go." I'd been a single mother with three small children, and I knew all too well how difficult it would be for her with five. I also knew how much easier it would be without Tal's restrictions and the certainty of another baby before she was recovered from this one.

The news must have gotten out, because a parade of sombre rabbis and serious-faced women from the Jewish community filed in and out of the basement during the next two weeks. I guessed they were trying to dissuade Miriam, but in her quiet way, she was stubborn. She told me Tal would be staying on after she left, which worried me. He still had no job, and his car had recently been repossessed. Their mail came with mine, and I couldn't help but notice the ever-increasing stack of windowed envelopes with *final notice* stamped across the front in red. It didn't bode well for the rent, and without Miriam around to clean, I was afraid the basement would soon resemble the city dump. Even getting Tal to take his copious garbage all the way out to the alley was a weekly challenge. I decided to give him notice, but not before Miriam left. I dreaded the confrontation. Because of his religious convictions, he assumed he was always right, and he tended to be bombastic.

I should have remembered that things have a way of working out.

Miriam was leaving on Sunday. On Saturday morning, my firefighter son arrived to do some plumbing for me. I'd long wanted taps in my bathroom that I could turn on and off with my foot, adding hot water as needed. Long, hot bubble baths are one of my fondest indulgences.

"I have to turn the water off at the main valve, and it's in the basement, in that room Tal uses as a study," Dan said. "He's going to go ballistic because it's Shabbat."

My sons, my friends, the neighbours—all of us were now overly familiar with Shabbat.

"I'll go warn Tal." I knew he wouldn't like it. I knew all

too well that in his view, no one should tinker with water on Shabbat. No one should work on Shabbat, or wash on Shabbat, or do anything except fornicate, I thought irritably. But Dan had to return to work the next day, so my window of opportunity was narrow, and visions of bubble baths sent me reluctantly down to Tal in his den.

He was wearing a freshly ironed white shirt, yarmulke and black dress pants, sitting in a rocking chair studiously studying a holy book when Miriam answered the door. The kids were subdued, Miriam pale and tired looking. Suitcases were everywhere, and Tal looked out of sorts. I told him about the water main, and he shook his head.

"It's Shabbat, no water on Shabbat."

"Dan only has today off," I wheedled. "All he'll do is turn the water off and then on again in an hour or so. It won't affect you at all. He's a fireman—he knows what he's doing."

Tal didn't agree, but he didn't outright forbid it, either. I told Dan to go ahead, retreated to my studio and was concentrating on Chapter Eight of the latest romance when the basement door burst open. Tal was the first to appear, as wet as if he'd jumped into a pool fully clothed. Dan was behind him, also soaked to the skin. Behind them came dripping kids one after the other, and finally Miriam with the baby, both of them likewise very wet.

"Water," Tal was shrieking, waving his arms and doing a demented dance in my garden. "Water everywhere, and its Shabbat. I told you no water on Shabbat."

"Get the fuck out of my way and shut up!" Dan hollered at Tal, obviously driven way beyond his courtesy level.

To me, standing aghast in the door of the studio, Dan shouted, "Quick, Ma, where's a long hose? The lever broke on the intake valve, the basement's flooding fast."

I pointed the way to my longest hose. Dan lopped off the end with a knife and disappeared back downstairs. I took Miriam and the kids upstairs and supplied towels, then ran down and started moving suitcases outside. Dan hadn't been exaggerating; the basement already resembled a wading pool, and even as I salvaged suitcases, the water deepened at an alarming rate.

Tal, totally useless at anything practical, was still circumnavigating the back garden, hands on his head, emoting about Shabbat and water and proclaiming what I assumed were curses in Yiddish, directed at Dan and I.

The older kids escaped Miriam, ignored their father, and came tearing back downstairs. They were elated because they now had a wading pool. They leaped and jumped about in the deepening water, laughing and having a wonderful time. Of course, Louie and Sammy joined the circus, peering into the basement, blocking the door, and generally impeding progress.

With great difficulty, Dan finally managed to get one end of the hose pulled over the spouting valve, and we ran the other end into the alley, pointing it down into the sewer drain. The force of the water coming in from the city was unbelievable.

"I have to dig up the front garden and find the main turnoff," Dan panted, racing in that direction with a shovel.

"Shouldn't I call the fire department and get them to come shut it off?"

"No!" Dan roared. "I'm a fireman. I'd never hear the end of it if the Department found out I flooded my mother's house. Call the emergency number at the City and find out where the damned shut off actually is."

My three sons are amazingly strong. Dan played World Rugby for five years, and he hadn't lost his conditioning. It took me fifteen minutes to finally get through the maze of the automated City switchboard and speak to a real human. In that time, Dan had dug a trench half way across the front of my garden, looking for the shut off. There was a pile of dirt two feet high all along the sidewalk.

The shut off turned out to be on the opposite end from where he was digging, so when I shouted out the right location, Dan started all over again. Within half an hour, he'd dug four feet down and three feet in from the sidewalk, found the shut off, and turned it off. By that time, we'd come near to flooding the storm drain in the alley, and every neighbour on both sides of the street was in front of my house, enjoying the matinee.

After the water was finally turned off, it didn't take long for Dan to repair the faulty connection and turn the water on again. He finished with my taps, filled in the holes in the front lawn and quietly warned me that from here on in, his career as a part-time plumber was over. I needed to put a certified plumber on standby. He put on the clean, dry clothes his wife had delivered and, tired to the bone, slunk off home.

Miriam had also found dry clothes for the kids in the suitcases I'd hauled upstairs. We washed and dried the wet things and I offered to pay for them all to stay at a hotel, but she'd already contacted a friend who came and picked them up. I apologized profusely, but Miriam quietly said she knew it was an accident. She didn't blame me at all. Tal, however, was a different matter. He was still fuming about water and Shabbat, and he informed me that all his suits, hanging in the closet in his room, had been ruined by the water. I gathered them up and took them to the cleaners. They were only slightly damp. The door to the closet had protected them.

"How am I going to live down there?" he whined. "There'll be mould and mildew. You'll have to lower the rent."

I took a deep breath. "I'm sorry, Tal, but you have to find another place to stay. I'm going to totally redo the suite, including digging a new sewer line which will allow for a regular toilet. It's going to take a long time. I'll reimburse you for this month's rent in lieu of adequate notice."

"You'll also have to pay for all my suits," he said in a sulky voice.

I didn't point out that the suits were at least ten years old and not exactly Armani. "The cleaner assured me there's no real damage to them. I'll pick them up on Monday. You can come by and check on them. If they're not as good as they were before, I'll make it up to you."

He finally slunk off, and I phoned the insurance people. They came immediately. It turned out the intake valve had been inadequately soldered, and so they'd cover the cost of repairs.

That night, I filled the tub with bubbles and each time the water cooled, I turned the hot tap on again with my foot and reviewed the day. It had been memorable. The bad news was that it had cost me a month's rent, a hefty cleaning bill and I'd owe Mavis another small fortune when she came to repair the extensive damage to the uprooted front garden. But the good news far outweighed the bad: I'd never have to consider Shabbat again when I blew a fuse or needed Eric to repair something on a Saturday.

Tal was no longer with me, Miriam was off to a new and—I hoped—less stressful life, and the insurance people would pay for the repairs caused by water damage. I'd miss the kids, particularly Leah, but I wouldn't have to worry about them falling into the pond or babysit them every Saturday afternoon.

The damned electric toilet was all but a thing of the past, and I'd be a lot more discerning when I next rented my basement suite. Dealing with long-term renters made running the Blue Collar B&B seem like child's play.

Tal came back two weeks later to pick up the suits, which even he, after a minute examination, had to admit were undamaged.

"Miriam and the children are in London on holiday," he told me. "I miss them, but they'll be back soon."

His eyes told a different story, however. Bleak and drained of hope, I guessed that he knew Miriam was gone for good, but he couldn't let himself admit it. He looked unkempt, his shirt not ironed, his suit rumpled. He hadn't shaved in days. I felt a rush of sympathy for him. Who among us hasn't made mistakes with dire consequences, not recognizing the need for dramatic change in our actions until it's too late? Learning shouldn't have to be painful, but it usually is. Obviously, it was for Tal.

He said, "I wondered if you'd rent me a room upstairs? I'm staying with a friend, and it's not working out."

"No." The unadorned word popped out without apology. Sorry for him or not, I, too, had learned my lesson the hard way. Tal and I were not compatible.

He left that day and I never saw him again. I received calls for weeks afterwards, asking for his address or phone number. It seemed he had debts all over town. Tal and his family had been an extreme learning experience for me. Guests may or may not be the most amenable folks around, but the fact is, they're only going to be with you for a limited time. Unless they're dramatically pregnant when they check in, chances are two guests are not going to become three or more overnight.

Their religious convictions rarely come under discussion, much less affect the life of the host. They don't ask if they can build shanties in the back garden. So far, none had assumed I'd babysit while they made whoopee.

The drama of that last day made me ponder the qualities of water. Nothing is softer and weaker when it's still. Nothing is more powerful when it's in motion. The more you attempt to hold on to water, the more it slips away. It seemed a powerful metaphor for Tal and Miriam's relationship.

As repairs downstairs progressed, I once again began to compose an ad for the suite. Political correctness forbade my saying so, but I was praying that I'd attract a quiet, gay, Buddhist couple who liked cats and meditated a great deal.

MY OWN FAVOURITE LITTLE MEDITATION
(I used it a LOT at this particular time)

Sit comfortably. Imagine yourself taking the hand of whatever ascended Being you feel at ease with. Go with them towards a beautiful golden light. Just before you reach it, there's an altar on your right. Take every damned thing that's bothering you, no matter how large or small or silly, and heap it all on. Tell the Creator how grateful you are to be made in Its image, to be forever safe and totally provided for. These are your gifts, because you would have no idols. Express your love, and watch your gifts disappear into the Light. And then be silent. Immerse yourself in the Light. Five minutes is plenty.

THE WHOLE HOUSE BEGAN TO TREMBLE, AND YOU FELT THE OLD TUG AT YOUR ANKLES

*(*Mary Oliver, *The Journey)*

My B&B guests came and left again in a more or less steady, pleasant stream, and one day I realized I'd been running the Blue Collar for five years. There comes a time for all of us when change is necessary, and something in me slowly became aware that that time was arriving for me. It began in my gut, as all forewarnings of change do. I had a vague sense of waiting, of something different this way comes. It was subliminal.

Deep in the Rocky Mountains of British Columbia, there's a beautiful valley where a small coal mining town called Sparwood nestles. A river runs through. It's called the Elk. The valley is also called the Elk, named for the abundance of wild game—elk, deer, bear, cougars, moose, lynx, beaver, and bobcat. The Elk River has Kokanee, the fabled inland salmon, as well as grayling and brook trout.

Rich in natural resources, timber, coal, and wild game, the area had remained virtually unknown until recently when a developer had an epiphany one morning while shovelling some of the area's average 379 inches of snowfall from his front walk. He saw the potential for a ski resort in nearby sleepy Fernie, which is at the confluence of three valleys where storms unload snow for days on end. He trusted his intuition. He built the resort, telling himself that they'd come, and come they did.

Soon skiers from all over the world travelled to Fernie to experience the abundance of long, steep fall-line skiing off the ridgelines, and there was a slow but steadily increasing spill over to Sparwood, twenty minutes north down Highway No. 3. Locals had almost stopped wearing tee shirts that said, *Where The Hell is Sparwood*.

I had always known where Sparwood was. For me, it was home, the place where I was born. My grandfather came here from Scotland with his sixteen-year-old bride in 1898. He got a job in the coal mine, and settled. Here, my father and his seven brothers and sisters were born. I was born here, and my brother Ole and my sister Karen. I even came back to the Valley to have my own first son, Dan. All my sons spent their summers here with my mom and dad, welcome respites from the troubled life they led in the city with their father, their stepfather, and me.

My family's roots go as deep in this valley as the seams of coal in the mountains. My father lived his entire adult life in the house he and my mother built, a few thousand meters from his parents' house where he was born. He was buried in the graveyard across from the trailer park where my middle son lived until he married Lisa. My mother lies beside my dad. She died more recently, and soon afterwards, my brother's wife, Gerry, joined them, a shock to us all because she was vibrant and young. She was fond of saying *whatever doesn't kill you makes you stronger*. My brother Ole was devastated when the rare blood disease killed her in two weeks. Unlike me, my brother and sister mated for life.

Ole and I were close in spirit, but hundreds of miles distant in reality. Both my sister Karen and my brother had married locals and never left the Valley. Their children had settled there, as had numerous cousins. Two of my sons, Dave and Rob, moved back to Sparwood with their wives. I was the renegade, the prodigal, the City Girl who lived Away. At eighteen, I'd married and moved, returning only for visits that increasingly centered around weddings and funerals. In my heart of hearts, I never dreamed I'd go back to the Valley on any sort of permanent basis. It wasn't that I didn't love it there, I did. It was, and would always be, my heart's home, but I needed a larger venue in which to grow—or so I'd always thought, until my most recent visit.

It was a sunny afternoon in June. My daughter-in-law Lisa and I were driving aimlessly around the Valley in a last ditch attempt to put my tired grandbabies to sleep. We'd wound down a hill to the bridge that crossed the Elk River. There was a clear view of the idyllic riverside acreage where my cousin Tommy lived in a long, low white house. A huge red barn and other outbuildings sprawled across the five acres, all of it river frontage, all of it treed.

"That place has been on the market for a while now," Lisa commented. "Somebody's missing a bet. It would make a perfect fishing lodge. The Elk is becoming famous for inland salmon. Fly fishermen are starting to come from everywhere to fish here, and they need places to launch their boats, somewhere to stay. That house is huge. Tommy's done lots of renovating and he's gone first class all the way. And the barn could be used to store float boats and maybe house a place where fishermen could come and buy bait."

"What's it listed for?"

"Five hundred thousand. Nobody here will pay that for it, though. Tommy's dreaming."

"Why is he selling?"

"Erna's not well, and she's never liked it there. She'd rather be in town."

And in that instant, the rest of my life came clear to me. I would sell my house in Vancouver, buy Tommy's place, and be the Queen of the Elk. Well, considering my age, maybe the Queen Mother.

Real estate in Vancouver was at an all-time high. My modest

house would probably sell in the low seven hundred thousands. I could pay off my mortgage, buy Tommy's acreage, and have some left over for renovations. I would be mortgage free, and I'd have more rooms to rent than I had in Vancouver, with a built-in clientele. I would be free once and for all of my crippling money worries and I wouldn't have to write three books a year. But I'd have to give up the Blue Collar just when I'd established a steady clientele. I'd leave behind the Lost Boys, my garden, my writing studio, Dan and his family, and my small circle of friends.

I'd lose my anonymity: I was related to half of Sparwood, and the other half had attended writing seminars I'd put on for the local library. I was a minor celebrity in my hometown, the first and only Sparwood High graduate to succeed as a novelist. I'd be closely watched and reported on every time I farted.

On the other hand, I wouldn't have Louie and Sam to contend with every day. Louie had become more and more difficult, appearing at my door sometimes seven or eight times a day, phoning me repeatedly if, God help me, I ignored the doorbell and hid in my room to escape him. He brought me gifts, flowers from my own garden, small kitchen things he didn't use, lottery tickets with his name scrawled across them—if we won, he'd tell me ad nauseum, we'd fly to England. He had a cousin in England and he wanted to see her before he died.

Poor man. I had compassion for him, but the daily strain of living next door to him was wearing me down. He made me promise a dozen times a week that if anything happened to him I would adopt Sam. That promise was my worst nightmare. The rotten cat had grown meaner with age, hissing at me when I squirted him with a water bottle to try and prevent yet another smelly deposit in my garden, then giving me what I was certain were gloating looks from the safety of Louie's arms.

He'd sneaked into my house countless times and used his claws on the furniture. I'd caught him sleeping in the guest bedrooms, on the beds, which meant washing the duvet covers to rid them of hair and cat odour. Sadly, I wouldn't miss Sam and Louie at all.

But there was the monumental physical effort required for moving. I had a four bedroom house full of furniture, a studio filled with electronic equipment, and a three bedroom furnished suite to dismantle. The very thought of packing up all that stuff gave me a headache, but then I reminded myself that I didn't have to pack it all in one day. I could work on just one box at a time. Most of this flashed through my mind in the time it took to put the babies to sleep in the car that afternoon.

That evening, I went to see my cousin Tommy. Just to look, I told myself, even though part of me knew I'd already made up my mind. He showed me his lovely house. It was spacious and beautifully renovated from the original farmhouse, with expensive appliances, old cedar floors underneath wall-to-wall carpet, three bedrooms and two baths up and enormous potential in the semi-finished dance hall sized area down.

Granted, it had a few oddities, like the huge hot tub that had never been used, squatting smack in the middle of the massive living room. Why, I asked, hadn't it ever been filled?

"Erna doesn't want the mess," Tommy explained.

That made sense. Erna was a fanatically clean housekeeper.

"Your water's sulphur." I could smell it the moment I walked through the back door.

"There's a water purifier." Tommy took me to inspect it. It was in a large, immaculate room where the electrical panels and other controls were, and it looked a bit like the control center in *2001, A Space Odyssey*. Without Hal.

There was electric baseboard heating throughout the house, but the major source of heat was a huge burner in the barn which gobbled up six foot lengths of logs and sent hot water coursing through the pipes in the house. That gave me pause, because when it was minus 35 Celsius I knew I would have to trek out to the barn to restock the burner. And there was the problem of the logs—they arrived as full length trees and Tommy cut them up. I'd have to hire someone to do that for me, or learn to use a power saw.

"The burner only needs refuelling once every twenty-four hours," Tommy assured me. "And the house is well insulated, it stays really warm. We're blood. I'll come and cut up logs for you."

I looked around with an eye to running a lodge, and there was no doubt the house was eminently suitable. The location was the major asset. The land sloped gently down to the river, and weeping willows lined the banks. I had visions of waking up in the morning to the sound of the water and the birds.

I'd have to put in bedrooms and another bathroom downstairs, but there was potential for at least eight spacious bedrooms. And the rough plumbing was in place. The view of the river was breathtaking from the front windows, which spanned the entire width of the house. There was a three car garage that could be subdivided into a studio, also overlooking the water. In my enthusiasm for the house, I forgot to take a look at the barn. I knew that Tommy, who distrusted lawyers and real estate agents, did everything on a handshake, and before I left, we came to an agreement on price and shook hands on the deal.

"When will you be moving out?" I knew he was going to build. I hoped he wouldn't say immediately because I had to close down the Blue Collar and sell my Vancouver house, which could take time.

"I'm not sure yet. I hope to start construction on my new house this fall."

It was July. I did some quick calculations in my head. "So next summer would work for possession?"

"Sure. Next summer."

And before I could quite catch up with myself, the deal was done. Of course I'd have to hire a surveyor, have a professional check out Tommy's house, and get things in writing. But basically, it was a done deal. I wanted to. I didn't want to. I was afraid. I was excited. Change and growth go hand in hand, but change is terrifying. A wise man once counselled, *Shift from fear to curiosity.*

That day, in that valley where I was born, fear was a raging dragon within me, but the curious part of me knew that coming home was not only right, but inevitable.

As Mary Oliver writes in her poem, *The Journey*:

One day you finally knew what you had to do and began, though the voices around you kept shouting their bad advice.

Back in the city, I had a crisis of indecision every single morning at 2 a.m.

What was I doing leaving my well-established B&B to move to the back of beyond? How did I know fishermen would find me? And what the hell did I know about fishing, or float boats, or bait? What if it cost me much more than I anticipated to have Tommy's house renovated? What if I couldn't sell mine for the amount I needed?

And most pressing of all, when would Tommy give me a firm moving date? I'd called him several times, but couldn't pin him down. He hadn't even started building his new house.

The Lost Boys figured I'd temporarily gone totally berserk and went AWOL until I came to my senses, all except Eric, who pointed out reasonably enough that real estate was rising, I could eventually make much more money if I waited, say, five years. I was beginning to think that's how long it would take Tommy to build a house and move into it.

My lawyer daughter-in-law was appalled. She warned that if I made this foolish move, I'd never be able to buy back into the Vancouver real estate market. She'd grown up in Sparwood. She reminded me of the long, cold winters, the lack of shopping.

"You'll have to drive to Calgary to even go to Ikea. The

closest Costco is two hours away, and you practically live at Costco. You're going to get there and find out you want to come back, and it'll be too late."

My guests, most of whom were now regulars, begged me to stay. They loved it at the Blue Collar, where would they go if I closed down? Why did I think I needed to move?

Only my two best friends, Pat and Bev, quietly advised me to follow that insistent voice deep inside which was urging me, in the face of almost everything logical, to move to Sparwood. They'd miss me, but in our mutual search for integrity, peace, joy and some meaning to this shmozzle, they felt I needed to pay heed to what my spirit was telling me.

"Trust your intuition," they urged. "You are the only one who knows what's right for you."

It was the same advice we'd given each other through three divorces. There was the time I went to Mexico on a holiday with Ron and fell madly in love with Roberto, the hotel manager. I used up a dozen phone cards that time, calling Pat and Bev at all hours of the day and night because Ron threatened suicide before he flew home alone, and Roberto turned out to be not just an alcoholic, but high on good quality pot most of the time. Still, he was a beautiful man, and I've never been sorry.

There was also that time I rode a pedal bike over the Pyrenees with a broken wrist, following a man I soon labelled Attila the Hun. I'd honestly believed a small inner voice was sending me on a pilgrimage. Pat and Bev were totally supportive. All three of us just conveniently forgot that a pilgrimage is not necessarily fun.

So sometimes our intuition wasn't all it was cracked up to be, but through every misadventure, our friendship never faltered, and somehow we came through each crisis stronger, wiser and with our funny bones not only intact, but raised to another level. (Although in the case of the Pyrenees, mine was in a cast for three months.)

Blue Collar B & B

I talked to a real estate agent just to get an idea of what was what. The news was good and bad.

Real estate was at an all-time high, and my west side address was a bonus. The garden and the studio were hot selling points, but in order to reap the full benefit of a top end sale, the house—a robin's egg blue—needed a coat of paint. The front stairway needed replacing. (I found myself wishing Donnie had gotten around to that before I dumped him.)

No matter how popular the Blue Collar had become, I couldn't sell the place as a business because I'd never had a legal license to operate a B&B. In my own defence, I'd tried hard to be legal, meticulously putting in fire extinguishers, metal wastebaskets, locks on the upstairs windows, baseboard lighting that led to the bathrooms, stupid maps on the back of every door clearly showing fire escape routes. There were only two—out the window, or down the stairs, and you'd have to be seriously challenged not to figure that out.

But Vancouver by-laws insisted I have two parking spaces on site in order to qualify for a license, and that killed the deal. It meant tearing down the studio and filling in the pond in the back garden, then covering Mavis's prize day lilies with cement and knocking a hole in my lovely red fence. I wasn't prepared to go to those lengths. I was fairly certain it would push Mavis over the edge and into psychosis.

I also knew that unless someone lodged a complaint, the city didn't bother closing down unlicensed B&Bs. Besides Louie and Sammy, I had the best neighbours in the world. They minded their business and turned a blind eye to mine, so I'd blithely operated the Blue Collar for five years on the shady side of the law. Meanwhile, the summer was half over, and I guessed that summer was the prime time for selling, if I was going to, with my garden in full bloom. I was increasingly restless. I'd made the decision to move to Sparwood and I wanted to get on with it.

At 2 a.m. one morning, I asked myself if I'd still move if I took Tommy out of the picture. I made a list of my other reasons for moving. Finances were at the top, with the promise of earning a living running a fishing camp and not having to write. My Sparwood family was next. They wanted me with them, and they'd been over the top enthusiastic and supportive and encouraging and eager. And less rational, but most insistent of all, was the ever-growing conviction in my gut that this was what I was meant to do at this point in my life, whether I knew exactly why or not. I kept reminding myself that we never know what anything is for. The urge to go home was becoming stronger with each day that passed.

But I didn't have Tommy's house to move into, and it didn't look as if it was going to happen anytime soon. And then an idea came to me in one of my freak-out sessions. Compared to real estate prices in Vancouver, houses in Sparwood were still dirt cheap. Maybe I could buy a fixer-upper of a house right now, hire my son David, who wasn't working at the moment, to renovate it with me, and then sell it at a profit in a year or whenever Tommy finally made a move. Chances were good I'd make money on the deal—Fernie ski hill was gradually pushing local property prices up. But it would mean two major moves instead of one. If I moved once, I could do it again, using my theory that the more a person did something, the better they became at doing it—even if it embodied their worst nightmare. Moving was not my favourite pastime.

I drove to Sparwood the following weekend and bought a house in an afternoon. It was fifty-six years old, ten years younger than me. It was a one storey, solidly built structure with a large, but unfinished, basement. There was a long porch at the back that could be enclosed to become a studio. The location was perfect, right in town. It needed a lot of upgrading, but the basement had high ceilings and the potential for three bedrooms, common area, and bath. There were another three bedrooms and bath on the main floor, although the bathroom needed renovating.

The lot was large, with six big pines bordering the front sidewalk. There was a pathetic looking lawn, overgrown and patchy. The back garden had a garage and no garden or fence. The space had been converted to a gravel parking lot, open to the alley. *Needs landscaping*, I marked on my to-do list with remarkable constraint. But the price was right. The house was listed at $134,000—ridiculously cheap by Vancouver standards. And the house numbers—124—added up to seven. My Vancouver address, 88, was also a seven (eight and eight, sixteen, six plus one, seven). And seven was a most beneficent number in Chinese numerology.

Obviously, it was pre-ordained that I have this place.

I had barely enough left on my line of credit to write the cheque for the down payment. I'd already used a hefty chunk on such mad extravagances as a new bathroom in the Vancouver downstairs suite, my city taxes, and an overrun on my income tax. But write the cheque I did, although I had a sinking feeling that before I was done, finances were going to become a pain in the butt. I'd have to either sell my Vancouver house in a hurry or somehow bridge financing. Oh well, it would all work out, I told myself, doing my best to trust.

Back in Vancouver, I talked to Paul, a real estate agent friend of Dan's.

"If you want full value and a quick sale, the best thing to do is hire a stager," he advised.

A stager? What the hell was a stager?

"They come in and tell you what needs done to get the most money out of your property. It'll cost about two hundred, but you'll get ten times that back." He gave me Elizabeth's card.

She was tall, glamorous and aggressively gay. "First of all, we'll need to store at least fifty percent of your furniture and books," she said in a matter-of-fact tone. "Houses look bigger without so much stuff. Take the bed and dressers and shelves out of the downstairs bedroom"—*my beloved bedroom*—"and turn it into an entertainment centre. We'll need to change all the light fixtures, put new covers on the wall plugs, take the pegboard down in the kitchen, redo that wall, paint the stairwell and touch up anywhere that looks grungy. The dining room could use a fresh coat of paint, ditto the upstairs hall."

I'd never before met anyone who actually said ditto.

"At least half of those books have to go."

Quick breath, onwards and upwards.

"Tear out the wall-to-wall carpeting in the living room and redo the old oak floors. Here's a card for a guy who's reasonable and good. You'll have to move out for a couple of days, the smell of the varnish is toxic. The garden and studio are perfect just as they are, except—is that old man with the cat related to you?"

I assured her Louis and Sammy were not blood; they just lived next door.

"When you have the open, make certain they aren't anywhere around. No offense, but knowing someone like that lives next door could seriously affect your sale."

I took the carefully written list she gave me, began at the top and worked my way down, putting the items in order of difficulty. Then I rearranged them, in order of whether or not I could accomplish them while still having guests at the Blue Collar. I needed every cent of income to afford the changes that Elizabeth suggested.

True to my vow to pack only one box at a time, I decided that painting the exterior of the house could take place while the B&B operated. I got quotes from several painters, and then a call from Peter Pan, aka Steve.

"Eric says you want to paint the house. I'll do it for you. I've got the ladders and scaffolding. What's the lowest quote you got on the job?"

I told him, knowing that Eric probably already had.

He gave me a figure considerably lower.

"You buy the paint and brushes. I'll start early Monday

morning."

"Have you ever painted a house before?" I didn't know much about it, but the professionals I'd talked to had mentioned a lot of prep work, repairing or replacing worn boards, cleaning the surface first, undercoating, protecting the landscaping.

"I painted my mother's house last summer."

I had reservations. I knew Steve was anal to a whacky degree, which meant the job would undoubtedly be done well, but I wondered about the prep.

"Of course I'll do all the undercoating and everything. I'll do a perfect job. What colour are you using?"

"York Harbor. It's a deep, rich, golden yellow, with cream trim. It's going to be my yellow submarine."

His face brightened. "So, so—you're not going to sell the house after—after all?"

"I am going to sell. But I get to enjoy it for however long that takes."

"Why do you want to leave?" There was a plaintive note to his voice.

"I'm not so much leaving as going towards. I want to go back to where I was born. I want to be close to my family. I want to start a fishing camp."

"That's what Eric said. That's kinda nuts, even for you. By the way, Eric's smitten with you. He's going to really miss you, we all are. Why don't you take us with you?"

I felt a pang of preliminary loneliness. What would I do for eccentricity without the Lost Boys?

"I would if I could. But I can't."

"Maybe we'll come visit you."

"I'd love that." And I'd love to see the reaction in redneck Sparwood when my strange friends piled out of Steve's old Cadillac, Eric in his bike helmet, Steve in his ancient shorts, Roger, who'd become the gayest of gays.

Monday morning, I was awakened at six by the sound of

ladders and Steve's loud, bossy voice. He'd brought with him a boy of about fourteen and an exotically beautiful, slender young woman, maybe in her twenties. They were both dark skinned, and neither was proficient in English. They smiled and murmured shy greetings as Steve introduced them.

"This is Pyra and her brother Outar."

"I'm Bobby. Where are you from?" I smiled at them and offered coffee and fresh scones.

Steve took over as spokesman. "They're visitors from Guyana. My church sponsored them, and I offered to give them a job and help them learn English."

I hoped that was all lovely Pyra was learning from Steve.

"Do they know how to paint?"

"I'll teach them. Painting isn't rocket science."

Maybe not, but it was my house they'd be experimenting on. I was feeling less and less confident about Steve and this house painting thing, but true to form, his obsessive compulsive nature saved the day.

I forgot there was only one way to do things—Steve's way. From my studio, I heard him ordering his minions around, making them do the job exactly as he wanted it done, making them redo whatever wasn't up to his exacting standards.

Soon, inevitably, Louie appeared with Sammy in his arms. One of the things I found endearing about Steve was his endless patience with Louie. I couldn't hear what they were saying, but Louie was following Steve as he worked, and I knew all too well that he'd be asking the same question over and over, then expounding on Sammy's bowels and diet. At least it was giving me a respite. But I was wrong. A few moments later, Louie knocked insistently on my studio door. I'd tried to impress on him that when the door was closed, I was working and not to be disturbed, but of course he forgot the rule every new day.

The moment I opened the door, he said, "Steve says you're moving. Are you moving? Why are you moving? You promised to take Sammy when I go. How can you do that if you're moving?"

I hadn't warned Steve that I was keeping my plans secret from Louie, at least until the For Sale sign went up. He'd obsess over it as he did over everything, asking me the same question a million times, and then a million and one.

As he was doing right now.

I could see he was really upset, his unshaven face screwed into an anxious knot.

"If you aren't here, who'll take care of Sammy when I go? You promised you'd take care of my boy, who'll take care of Sammy if you move? You know Sammy really owns this place. What'll happen if he doesn't like the new people?"

What could I say? From Louie's point of view, I was a traitor or worse, reneging on a sacred vow.

"I'm not moving for a while, Louie."

"How long?"

It was July. "I'm not sure. Probably not until October." Hopefully. October first was the closing date on the Sparwood house. I'd spoken to my bank manager, and she'd reluctantly agreed to bridge financing, but only for a month. And the interest was astronomical. I felt dizzy every time I thought about my precarious financial situation.

"Maybe Sammy can go with you. Will Sammy like it where you're going?"

I drew in a calming breath. "Sammy would be miserable away from you, Louie. He needs to stay with you."

"Yes, but after I go? You'll take him after I go?"

There were times when he tried my patience beyond reason. "You're perfectly healthy, Louie, you're not going anywhere. It'll be a long time before you have to think about it."

He nodded. "Mother lived to a hundred and two."

"Yes, and longevity is inherited, so like I say, you'll be around a long time."

"Steve says he'll paint my steps, my steps need painting."

"That's really kind of Steve."

"I like Steve. Steve's not married. I've decided not to get married."

"Wise decision. Now I have to work."

I closed the door on him as he let Sammy down. The cat watched me watching him, gave me a snide look, and then went into a three-point stance and took a poop right in the middle of my path.

TIPS FROM A HOME STAGER

- *Pack away all personal mementos and photos. Buyers are not interested in your grandchildren or ex-husbands. The house should resemble a show home—tour a few to get the idea.*

- *Clean out the cupboards and closets, removing at least half of the kitchen stuff and ¾ of the clothing. Less makes the space look like more. Take everything off the countertops except the microwave.*

- *Paint the entire interior a neutral off white—or my favourite, lambskin duvet, a shade between white and cream. Uniformity produces a palette against which your few remaining pieces of furniture look elegant.*

- *Buy the most luxurious looking new white bed coverings you can afford, ditto for new towels for the bathrooms. (The stager will suggest colour schemes, but white is always good.)*

- *Change all the light fixtures if they're old but not classy. Same with the shower heads; rain shower heads are the way to go.*

- *Examine the house from the front sidewalk and be ruthless* as to curb appeal. If necessary, hire a gardener to shove in some greenery or flowers. The posts holding up my tiny front porch roof looked too small, for example. We used boards to fake in new, more substantial beams. A coat of paint and they looked as if they'd always been there.

- *If you have an attic, clean it thoroughly and get rid of any vermin traps you might have hanging around. Prospective buyers are weird about crawling into crawl spaces and squeezing into attics.*

- *Don't take the stager's comments personally. She's interested in a sale for a whopping amount, just as you are. This house is no longer an extension of your unique personality. It's a product for which sentiment has no place, and appearance is everything.*

How crass, how shallow. How financially beneficial.

I BROKE THE LID OF MY CHEST OPEN AND WAS STARTLED INTO FINDING MY OWN WEALTH

*(*Rabindranath Tagore*)*

The house painting progressed with fewer calamities than I'd anticipated. There was the morning when one of Steve's ladders poked through the upstairs window screen at 6 a.m. and frightened a timid visiting school teacher into a screaming fit, but that was all the indignity any of my guests suffered.

Steve drove the poor Guyana visitors mercilessly, even though Eric confided that lovely Pyra was Steve's latest conquest, just as I'd feared. I watched her trying desperately to please him, giving him longing looks, bringing him fancy lunches, and I amused myself by speculating on what the universe might have in store for Steve next time around. A hopelessly unattractive female body, one could only hope? Or just a series of unrequited love affairs, with a heart broken over and over again? Or maybe, in this very lifetime, he'd fall hopelessly in love with a woman immune to his particular charms. It's always comforting to know that karma is impartial and inevitable—except when one applies it personally.

With the first coat of rich yellow, the house took on a festive, cheerful air that it lacked when it was blue. With the addition of cream trim on fascia boards and down pipes, my old house began to look positively elegant, rather like an impeccable lady of a certain age with a sense of humour.

Inside, I patched scratches and small holes on my walls, becoming an expert with spackle. I painted and began to pack up boxes of books and knick-knacks.

The day arrived in late August when I booked my very last guests—Patrick and Christine from Eugene, Oregon. I asked, as I always do, what work they did, what they wanted from life, what they needed from me to make their stay comfortable.

"I worked in the film industry," Patrick said. He named a string of well-known films he'd co-directed. "But now I'm retired, I spend most of my time fishing."

I'm always amazed at the serendipity of life. I explained that I was leaving Vancouver to start a fishing lodge in Sparwood, and he immediately offered to publicize my lodge in the best of the fishing magazines in exchange for a weekend's lodging.

"The Elk River is well-known among fly fishermen, you'll do really well," he said, and my heart soared. It was the first practical indication I'd had that the move would be successful, and I was grateful. It was heartening to have the fishing seal of approval on my intention to become the Queen of the Elk.

When Patrick and Christine left, I began ticking off the chores Elizabeth had detailed.

Gordon, the huge bear of a man who redid cedar floors, came with two young helpers and ripped out my carpeting after Eric and I and Steve somehow, with superhuman determination, managed to move all the living room furniture into the other rooms. Now it wasn't possible to even walk through the dining room. There were sofas, tables, and armoires stacked to the ceiling. There was also a nasty surprise under that old living room carpeting. There must have once been a wall across the middle of the room. Someone had taken it out and replaced the gaping hole in the floor with fir, which didn't at all match the rest of the wood.

"I'll have to find some old cedar flooring and replace that," Gordon told me. "So the job's going to take longer and cost a lot more."

"Okay," I croaked. I'd have to start getting advances on my credit cards. I was praying hard and frantically that the house would sell fast. Knowing that like attracts like, I did what I could to convince myself that I was wealthy.

On a book of old cheques, at two every morning, I wrote myself ever-increasing amounts, going up by tens of thousands every night. Then I wrote down exactly how I'd spend it, taking my entire family to Mexico, paying off every debt any of us had, putting money into trust funds for college educations should my grandkids want that. Buying good jewellery, setting up a shelter for battered women, adopting every one of the sad orphaned kids they show on TV. By the time I was up to a couple million, I'd run out of things to buy and do. But I'd fall asleep feeling wealthy, and the ache in my stomach would have disappeared.

Gordon, the wooden floor man, was a quick worker. In three days, he'd replaced the fir with cedar, stripped the floor, sanded it down, gradually putting on three coats of something so noxious I gagged and got dizzy each time I walked in.

I ate at the White Spot and slept in the studio. For the first time in years, I had nothing to do but take care of myself, write, and increase my imaginary income whenever a fit of the awful awfuls struck. Gordon took to coming out and having tea with me and, inevitably, telling me the story of his life.

He'd worked at refinishing floors all his life, and he loved what he did, reclaiming original damaged wood and making it beautiful. He'd gone from doing the work all himself to having two employees, then four, then ten, then twenty-seven. He formed a company and found himself spending all his time supervising crews and keeping track of the books, and for the first time, he began having complaints about his work. His blood pressure went up. His sex drive went down. His temper escalated.

"Employees are never gonna do the same job you'd do yourself, right?" he said, punctuating his words with expressive hand gestures. "I mean, they're workin' by the hour, right? Ya can't blame them for takin' shortcuts. But I started to hate goin' to work every morning."

And then the unimaginable happened. Gordon and his wife won the lottery, big time.

"I closed the company down. We went to Hawaii for a coupla months. Then we went to Europe. And I got fed up with doin' nothin', I tell ya. So we came home and I bought an old house just for fun, to redo the floors, and would ya believe, the little man started ta make his presence known. Goddamn, it felt so good. Sold that house, and then started right where I'd been years ago, workin' with a couple helpers doin' contract work on a small scale. Been doin' that ever since, and I tell ya, I'm one happy guy. Don't take no jobs for people I don't like, don't have to. The missus is all for it. I wasn't so nice to live with when I wasn't workin'. Or when I was a big time entra-pen-oor, neither."

I remembered the advice the Junkman had given me about buying the house next door and expanding. I thought of the eight rooms I'd be renting out at Tommy's. That could mean sixteen people for breakfast. I'd also been flirting with the idea of putting up yurts along the riverbank and renting them out, starting a fishing supply store in the barn, buying a couple of float boats, maybe offering to do lunches for groups. I'd need more than a few employees. I needed to think carefully about all my dreams.

For me, Gordon's story was a cautionary tale. Just as my women friends and I had concluded years ago, maybe bigger wasn't necessarily better. It's something the aspiring bed and breakfast host needs to take under careful consideration.

HOW TO FEEL WEALTHY WHEN YOU'RE EMPHATICALLY NOT

What your current financial circumstances are is not nearly as important as how you feel about them. Like attracts like, so by feeling desperate and lacking and impoverished, that's what the universe, being totally impartial, sends back. So we need to change the way we feel, we need to feel abundant, as if we're receiving abundance and money instead of lacking it.

Play a little game with me.

Go beg, borrow or steal (joking) a hundred dollar bill and put it in your wallet. Keep it with you, feel wealthy with it there. Now, as you go through your days, notice and take note of the myriad ways you could spend it. (If you actually bought the first thing you thought of, you'd get the vibrational feeling of wealth and abundance only once.) But if you pretend to spend it forty or fifty times a day, you increase that vibration to having spent four or five thousand dollars. You think, yup, I could have that—yes, I can have that. Zowee, that's possible. And because you do have the ability to buy any of those things—the $100 is right there—you're not pretending something that doesn't exist. There's no doubt getting in the way of the financial flow. There'll be a vibrational shift from impoverished to abundant, and—trust me on this, I've used it often—your income will overwhelm your outgo. (If you need to think bigger, use a $500 dollar bill.) I haven't actually really even seen one of those, but hey! Go for it.

What've you got to lose?

WORDS ARE A VIRUS FROM OUTER SPACE

(Song by Lorey Anderson)

Methodically, charge card in hand at Ikea and Home Depot, I waded through Elizabeth's list. I was packing up the things she'd suggested I store and then shipping them to Sparwood. My Sparwood son, Rob, would supervise putting them into a storage facility. So I bought packing boxes and filled them, fifty-three with books alone. I rented a five ton U-Haul. Eric and I loaded it to the gunnels, and then Dan drove it to Sparwood, where he and Rob unloaded it into storage.

My sons phoned me that night to tell me I had way too much stuff, which I knew all too well. The problem was, I'd be moving into an even larger house, I reminded them, and I'd need every mattress, bed, and armoire.

"The books, Ma. Do you really need all those books?"

I did. My collection of books was for research, I assured them. It was, but my book fetish went way beyond research. I'd learned to read at five, and it remains the mega passion of my life. My father was a coal miner and we were poor. We didn't own any books. But we had rich neighbours, Mr. and Mrs. Lazaruk. They were rich because they could afford bananas, and they had a full set of outdated Britannica encyclopedia they'd bought from a travelling salesman.

I loved the bananas Mama Lazaruk fed me, but I coveted those books. My mom and dad spent every Saturday evening playing whist with the Lazaruk's, and sitting in the corner of a horsehair sofa beneath a dim light, I read my way through from A to Z. I determined that when I grew up, I'd buy books, and I had. Every room in every house I lived in had overflowing bookshelves. I gave books away, but never in the quantity I accumulated them. I had to admit the house felt lighter without so many volumes, but I wasn't about to admit that to my sons.

The floors were spectacular. I didn't have a lot of time to enjoy them because there were two million and seven details to see to. I worked frantically, from dawn to dusk, making every room a showpiece, changing lighting fixtures, exposing brick, sanding, and cleaning windows. And every time I turned around, in the middle of every job, Louie was at the door with another gift: flowers from some absent neighbour's garden; used postcards; outdated telephones (he had a fixation with telephones and cameras); dozens of photographs of Sam; photographs of me reading in the tree house, lounging in the hammock, bending over wearing shorts to see if there were any fish left in the pond. God, was that actually my behind? I hadn't known he'd taken these, of course.

"I could take some of you in your underwear," he generously offered. "I used to be an underwear photographer, you know."

"Louie, thank you, but no. And no more gifts," I repeated like an old, shredding mantra, trying to curb my growing irritation. Anger is never justified, I reminded myself.

"I have to pack everything, there's no room."

I should have saved my breath to cool my porridge, as my father used to advise. Louie paid no attention, and Sam took to sneaking in and skating around on my newly finished floors, hissing at me when I chased him with a broom. Gordon warned it would take three weeks for the finish to harden, and Sam's claws were leaving faint scratch marks. I fantasized over a thousand

and two ways to put that cat down.

The day of my open house arrived. I was up at five arranging flowers in every room, cleaning the bathroom after I showered, not daring to even have a cup of tea in the pristine kitchen. Not that I wanted one; my stomach was sick with nerves. All my hopes and plans hinged on a quick and successful sale. If only it would happen today, without weeks of open houses, sleepless nights writing myself checks, and days spent trying to make the place look like a comfortable family home where nobody actually lived.

I was spending the day with my grandsons, and as I headed out to my car past the sign that read *Open House Today, Ten to Four,* Louie popped out his front door, the cursed cat cradled in his arms.

"I'll make sure all the people that come know Sammy thinks he owns your house," he promised. "He'll make sure the right people buy it from you."

That old romance cliché actually happened—my heart sank.

"I think you should keep him inside today, Louie. Someone could steal him, you know."

Louie laughed. "Nobody could steal Sammy. They'd be sorry. He'd scratch them and fight, wouldn't you, little boy?"

Louie and the demon cat were surely going to screw up my sale. Wanting to bawl from sheer frustration, I climbed in the car and drove away. But all my fears were groundless, as fears usually are. There were three solid offers that day, and they developed into a bidding war. My house sold to a young lawyer, a single father, for substantially more than its list price, nearly double what I'd paid for it five years before. And the closing date was mid October. My money worries were all but over.

I bought still more boxes and now the packing took on a frenzied quality, but inside I was filled with amazement and gratitude, if not peace. Not quite yet. Just like the man who's been imprisoned in a dark cave for years and suddenly is free, I couldn't immediately take in my windfall or really feel elated over it. So much to do, so little time, less than a month before I'd be leaving, then three weeks, then two, then twelve days, and that was the day Louie rang the doorbell for the fifth time that hot afternoon.

I was feeling particularly harassed. I'd run out of boxes again, there was a problem with the truck I'd pre-ordered from U-Haul, my credit cards were all maxed out, and the guy who'd bought the house kept phoning with impossible questions like what were the exact dimensions of the dining room, and would I measure it please to see if his dining table would fit. He'd dropped by numerous times with his kids, who rampaged through the house arguing over which rooms would be theirs. I was happy they loved the place, but I hadn't really said goodbye yet. I sort of wished they'd wait. And now here was Louie, holding a mason jar filled with faded artificial flowers which he'd undoubtedly lifted from the nearby graveyard.

"Sammy got these for you," he began. "You'll still take him with you if something happens to me, right?"

For the first time in five years, I totally lost it with him. My voice rose, and I spoke to him in a way I'd never done before.

"Take the flowers and go home, Louie. I mean it, you have to stop coming over all the time. I can't accept anything you bring. I've told you time and again I'm packing, and there's no room for anything else. I really don't have time for this. No more gifts, absolutely no more. *Go home.*"

I closed the sliding door in his face and locked it. He stood there for several minutes, and I hardened my heart against the shock and transparent hurt on his sagging face. A sad little voice in my heart reminded me that Louie was the most innocent of victims, that he was a part of me I didn't want to acknowledge. But I turned away, and finally I heard his shambling, shuffling progress down the deck stairs, mumbling to Sammy.

Blue Collar B & B

I felt guilty and mean and small-souled and terribly wrong, but there was too much to do to dwell on my shortcomings. I'd talk to him later, I decided. Right now I had to drive through the afternoon rush hour traffic to buy more packing boxes.

About seven that evening, I saw Louie slowly walking down the sidewalk. He went into his house, and for a moment, I thought of going after him, apologizing for my bad temper that morning. But I was exhausted and sweaty. I didn't have an hour to spend listening to him replay his familiar tapes about Sammy and marriage and women's underwear.

I filled the tub and revelled in a cool bath instead.

I read for several delicious hours, and when I finally went to bed, I noticed that Louie's kitchen light was on, which was unusual. He was meticulous about any routine once he'd mastered it, and he was always in bed with Sammy, lights out, by ten.

I got up to pee in the night, and the light was still on.

I was awakened from a deep sleep at six thirty the next morning by voices and unusual activity next door. I lurched to the open window. An ambulance and a coroner's removal van were in front of Louie's house. While I was trying to digest that, the front door opened and two attendants carried out a stretcher with a gray blanket covering a body.

Louie was dead.

My heart hammered, my ears rang, and I could hardly breathe. "I'm sorry, Louie, I'm so sorry," I babbled as remorse and regret overwhelmed me and the tears came.

Caroline knocked on my door moments later. She, too, was crying.

"I noticed the light on when I got up this morning," she said. "I came over and he was sitting in the kitchen with his head down on the table. The medical examiner thinks he died some time last evening. He'd been to the doctor in the afternoon. I didn't even get any phone call from the doc that might have warned me. Louie always had some minor thing wrong with his

heart, but nobody expected him to die anytime soon."
I could only think of the smartass quote I repeated when anyone talked about death. I couldn't remember where I'd read it, but it stuck in my head:

> We ought to have the date of our death stamped on our forehead. We'd live very differently.

So would those around us.

I asked Caroline, "What's going to happen to Sam?"

"He'll have to go to the SPCA. I have the dogs, I can't keep him.'

"I'll take him." I had to. I'd promised Louie.

She didn't argue. She didn't like the cat anymore than I did.

There was no service for Louie, only a private cremation. Caroline said he'd never belonged to a church, and of course, he had no other close friends. I missed the closure of a funeral. Knowing he could hear me, I told him repeatedly how sorry I was for that last day. I'd finish off with, "I'll take good care of Sammy, Louie. I promise."

Sammy was my penance, and he went out of his way to remind me of that fact.

Being fed tins of common cat food on my back steps wasn't that cat's idea of a good time, and for several days, he refused to eat, caterwauling his displeasure so the whole neighbourhood would know I was mistreating him. Caroline told me he was used to fresh lobster and shrimp from the fish market at Oakridge, and that he'd grown up eating off a plate, standing on the table right beside Louie. There was no way I was going to continue that madness. He'd just have to get used to the back porch and Nine Lives Tuna.

Fortunately, he still believed he lived at Louie's, so he used the cat door and presumably slept on Louie's bed, although he spent more and more time sunning himself on my deck. I imagined he was lonely, and for Louie's sake, I tried to make friends, but Sam would have none of it. We'd been adversaries for too long. I put a cat box by the back door for him, but he went on defiantly using my back garden as his toilet and hissing at me when I made half-hearted overtures.

The drive from Vancouver to Sparwood was at least twelve hours, and to say I wasn't looking forward to spending that time trapped in the car with Sam was an understatement of monumental proportions.

For the few remaining days before I left Vancouver, I'd startle awake every night at, oh, dark hundred, certain I'd just heard Louie's nasal voice in my garden, calling, "Sammy, Sammy. Come here, Sammy. Where are you, little boy?" I'd stagger out of bed and look out the window, expecting to see the old man out there in his pajamas, fly gaping, looking for that miserable cat.

I never did see him, but I told myself that didn't mean he wasn't there.

WHAT TO DO ABOUT REGRETS

So you can forgive everyone else in the dream—but not yourself. How arrogant is that? What makes you any different than any of the other dream figures? You are no worse, no more or less important, and certainly no better. Get over yourself.

If the person you feel you've wronged is gone from your immediate (so called) reality, like Louie was, then sit right down and write them a letter. Say your truth, admit your mistake, apologize. Express your love, they'll get the message. And for heaven's sake, move on, knowing that this, too, was just a lesson, and the other person has done you an immense service by reminding you that you aren't yet enlightened. (Damn it all anyway.)

MIRACULOUS BEINGS COME RUNNING TO HELP

(Zero Circle, by Rumi*)*

It was my final day. It was time to say goodbye to the Blue Collar. Everything was packed. Early the following morning, David and I would pick up the rented five ton truck. He and I, along with Dan and the Lost Boys, plus several of their dubious friends, would spend the day loading it. Dave would drive it over to Dan's where we'd spend the night, and then we'd leave before dawn. All I had to do today was find a suitable travelling cage for the bloody cat.

The doorbell rang just as I plugged the kettle in for tea that morning. It was the new owner of the house, shuffling from one foot to the other, looking hesitant and sounding embarrassed.

"Hi, Kevin. Come on in."

"I can't, thanks. I'm on my way to work." He took a deep breath and let it out in a whoosh of words.

"Bobby, I know this probably isn't possible, and it's asking a lot, but I promised my kids I'd ask anyway. See, they've fallen in love with your cat, Sammy. I spoke to the woman who's cleaning out the old guy's house next door, the old guy that had him before you? Louie, I think his name was? We met him the day of the open house. Anyway, she said he died and the cat belongs to you now. I don't suppose there's any possibility you'd consider letting us have him? I mean, I know how attached a person gets to a pet, and the old guy was your friend and all, so there's sentimental value. But, I just wondered—I mean, Sammy seems to like this house, he'd feel at home with us. And I've heard that cats don't always take well to moving. I promise you, we'd take really good care of him." His voice trailed off.

I had to use real discipline to keep myself from screaming *Halleluiah* and beating a tambourine while I ran naked through the streets, overcome with rapture. I cleared my throat and tried not to smile too wide. "Kevin, I think that's a great idea. Sammy would be much more settled if he stayed here. I'm so glad your kids like him."

"Really?" His grin split his face, and he punched a fist into the air. "*Yes!* God, the kids will be so happy, I can't tell you. Thank you *soooo* much."

"It's my pleasure." He had no idea how immense that pleasure really was.

I went out that day and bought two bottles of very nice wine and one of sparkling apple juice, along with a card welcoming Kevin and his kids to their new home. And then I spent a quiet few moments with the Gods of Irony in my garden. I couldn't hear their wings or their laughter, but I didn't have to. Let me tell you, they were there.

WORDS OF WISDOM FROM MY FRIEND PAT

Just do nothing.

ALL THE WORLD'S A STAGE, AND ALL THE MEN AND WOMEN MERELY PLAYERS

*(*Shakespeare, *As You Like It)*

Like fitting together a mathematical equation, Dan packed the last tiny space in the truck with the last of my belongings and shut the sliding rear door. The Lost Boys and their friends hugged me tight, promising to come and visit. I knew they never would; they never left the Lower Mainland.

Eric wrote down his pager, home phone, and cell number in a new leather covered address book and gave it to me. He knew how I lost phone numbers. We both were close to tears. We embraced once more, long and tight, and then he mounted his bike and rode away, red helmet glinting in the sunlight.

Everyone left. Dave drove the loaded truck across the city to Dan's, while I stayed behind for my private farewell to the Blue Collar. I walked slowly through the empty bedrooms where guests had made love, slept, made plans, dreamed dreams. I paused in the kitchen where I'd cooked so many breakfasts, the dining room where new friends from all over the world had sat around my table and sampled my quirky offerings. They'd laughed and cried and told me the secrets of their heart. They'd trusted me, thanked me, left me gifts—some more welcome than others—but each had taught me so many lessons.

This had been my stage. The players were my teachers and my students, as we all are to one another, and I was grateful to them.

I sat one last time on the back steps and looked out on the garden, the pond, the studio. Sam was nowhere around, and for the first time ever, I missed him. The house next door, like the Blue Collar, was stripped and empty, waiting for whatever the next act would bring.

And so was I.

THE TIME HAS COME, THE WALRUS SAID, TO TALK OF MANY THINGS

(The Walrus and the Carpenter, Lewis Carroll*)*

There is a hodgepodge of incidental minutiae the aspiring bed and breakfast hostess should know. I'm including them all here, in no particular order.

Cleanliness goes without saying, but I'll say it anyway. Guests at the Blue Collar shared a bathroom, and when more than one person was staying, I cleaned it several times a day, changing towels and washcloths, scouring out toilet and basin and tub, wiping up hair.

Hair is a big problem. I had more than a few guests who seemed to be losing it in handfuls. I found the best way to clean hair from shower stall and tub is with a moistened paper towel and magnifying glasses if necessary. The cardinal rule for the well-run B&B is: *Absolutely no short and curlies*! I relied heavily on bleach as a disinfectant.

Ditto with bathrooms—for some reason, (hair again, probably) guests don't like using bar soap. The dispenser type is a better choice. There are one-stop dispenser containers of liquid soap which can be used for bubble baths, shampoos, and body wash—I found them the best solution.

Stocking the bathroom drawers with a hair dryer, disposable

razors, and new travel packs of toothbrushes and toothpaste, as well as small bottles of bubble bath, is a good idea. Guests appreciate it.

Stores like Winners and TJ Maxx are a godsend for soaps, towels, bedding, even specialty jams and jellies. I suggest you remove the labels on the condiments and substitute a hand lettered one of your own. Mine read, for instance, Blue Collar Fig Jam, Blue Collar Plum Jelly, Blue Collar Bumbleberry Conserve. No one ever questioned the authenticity, and I figured it made guests feel pampered to think I'd spent hours slaving over a hot stove in the kitchen boiling down syrup to make them a delicacy. I don't see this as dishonest. Devious, maybe. But if it adds to the ambience and makes just one person happier for a few innocent moments, would the Pope object?

In the bedrooms, I used bedding made of natural fibres as much as possible, but there were always those few difficult guests who'd swear they were allergic to cotton or wool or feathers. One of these, a gentleman purportedly so rich he could have bought North America, (according to him, which again begs the question of why he was staying with me,) insisted he couldn't use my goose down duvet; he was highly allergic to feathers. I substituted a polyester quilt, forgetting all about the feather bed topper on the mattress. He slept on it very peacefully for six nights, telling me he was having the best rest of his life. I'm not saying there aren't genuine, bona fide allergies out there that must be addressed—I'm just commenting on one incident.

There are small services guests appreciate. If breakfast was to be at eight, I prepared trays at seven with coffee and/or tea in insulated carafes, with cream, sugar, and glasses of pure juice, and set the tray outside the guest's door, to enjoy as they performed their morning ablutions.

(Or not—I found a small number of guests came down to breakfast wearing the terry robes I supplied, eyes still glued shut with sleep dust, hair matted, bodies unwashed.) My mother would have sent them marching smartly back up to the bathroom to wash thoroughly, but then Mom wasn't charging for the rooms.

Bottles of water in each room, or glass jars of same, are a necessity. Occasionally, if guests were honeymooners or celebrating a special birthday or anniversary, I'd take them a bottle of wine in a cooler filled with ice, along with stemmed glasses. A ten dollar bottle of wine buys a million dollars worth of good will.

I always left a small plate of homemade cookies (usually my oatmeal chocolate chip, they seemed the most popular) in each room.

After finding out too late that guests preferred tea or chocolate to coffee, porridge to ham and eggs, or were diabetic and couldn't eat my muffins, I came up with a menu.

"Here's a little test for you," I'd tease, handing them the sheet of paper shortly after they were settled in. It looked like this, and the aspiring host is free to use it as a pattern.

WELCOME TO THE BLUE COLLAR

Here's a little quiz for you:

Do you prefer—

- ☐ Tea?
- ☐ Coffee?
- ☐ Herbal Tea?
- ☐ Decaf Coffee?
- ☐ Cream?
- ☐ Milk?
- ☐ Sugar?
- ☐ Chocolate?

Blue Collar B & B

Any food allergies? Diabetic? Vegetarian? Raw foods only?

What time would you like breakfast?

Do you fancy: (check off choices)

- ☐ Pancakes (sweet potato, buttermilk, blueberry)
- ☐ Cold Cereal with benefits (nuts and seeds on the side)
- ☐ Hot Irish oatmeal
- ☐ Blue Collar Mush
- ☐ Overnight groats
- ☐ Eggs (any style)
- ☐ Potatoes (also any style)
- ☐ French toast
- ☐ Bacon (or ham)
- ☐ Waffles
- ☐ Two egg omelette, French fashion
- ☐ Three egg omelette, Bobby fashion (same as French, only 3 eggs)
- ☐ Bobby's Green Energy Drink

La grande chef will do her best to fill any other requests. (Results not guaranteed.)

Any combination or (GASP) ALL OF THE ABOVE, God help me???

There are always fresh muffins and—or—scones, fresh fruit salad, and sometimes some wacky concoction the cook just felt like making.

ENJOY YOUR STAY!

WHILE YOU WERE SLEEPING

Breakfast, as in *Bed and,* is either a host's triumph or her downfall. In the manic pace of modern society, it's a meal much maligned and even totally ignored much of the time, which is probably why my guests spent more time than I would have thought possible poring over my menu, gleefully checking off one thing after the other, usually items that they didn't have the time to make at home.

This is why I crawled blearily out of bed a good two hours before their chosen breakfast time, made myself as presentable as possible and set feverishly to work in the kitchen baking, sautéing, pre-boiling, frying and generally making one hell of a mess of the counters and my clothing.

It was a shock to find out that the wacky things I included on the menu tongue in cheek were the ones most frequently requested, like Blue Collar mush and Bobby's Green Energy Drink.

Following are the recipes I found guests most enthusiastic about. They're also the ones that turned out faithfully, despite my early morning brain sputters.

First, the muffins and scones that were staples, always served warm on a pretty cloth napkin in a basket, in addition to guests' other choices.

Blue Collar B & B

BLUE COLLAR SCONES

4 cups unbleached flour
3 ½ teaspoons baking powder
1 teaspoon salt
¼ cup sugar
1 cup raisins or currants or blueberries,
or dried cranberries, or whatever else you fancy

Sift dry stuff together:
Add currants or whatever dried fruit you choose

Make a well in centre, add:
1 ¾ cups milk and ¼ cup oil

Stir enough to moisten, turn out on floured board and knead a few minutes. Make a big ball, cut in two. Flatten with hands to about ¾ inch circle, cut into six wedges. Ditto with other dough ball. Put on sheet pan, bake in preheated 450°F degree oven for 12 minutes.

When I got older and smarter, I made up a bucket of muffin batter to keep in the fridge for those mornings when even the thought of separate ingredients made me woozy. (Or when my exuberant guests had ordered so many menu choices I needed six arms or—my private fantasy, never fulfilled, alas—a muscular, not so young, virile male au pair to assist me, ahem.)

Bobby Hutchinson

THE BLUE COLLAR'S BUCKET FULL OF BATTER

In a smaller bowl:
Pour 2 cups boiling water over 2 cups 100% bran and let stand while you search for the rest of the stuff

In a gigantic bowl:
Cream 3 cups sugar into 1 cup butter

Add 4 eggs and beat the hell out of it.

Add buttermilk and bran mixture.

In yet another bowl:
sift flour, soda, salt and add to bran flakes.

(Yes, you need both kinds of bran. Your guests' bowels will appreciate this.) *Fold dry into wet, mixing slowly until well conglomerated. Store in airtight container in fridge for at least 24 hours before baking, at which time you can scatter some raisins, dates, or blueberries in if you feel up to it. Bake as many or as few as you like in a preheated 400°F degree oven for 15 to 20 minutes. This will make six dozen quite good, fluffy muffins and will keep up to six weeks.*

I also always served fresh fruit salad, in nice little stemmed dishes. Following is the Blue Collar secret to luring big gruff rednecks, male or female, into devouring the stuff.

Blue Collar B & B

BLUE COLLAR FRUIT SALAD

Peel and cut up, per guest:
About 1 cup of any combination of fresh fruit

Add:
A good sprinkling of nutmeg
A small slog of pure maple syrup
(About a teaspoon per serving)
Enough grapefruit juice to moisten
(And—here's the secret ingredient—*a generous slurp of Cointreau or any other fruity liqueur*)

Mix well, let marinate for a few minutes. Spoon into stemmed glassware, top with a sprig of mint or basil, and watch as they gobble it up.

Now, on to the main events guests requested most often.

Bobby Hutchinson

BLUE COLLAR MUSH

In a pot with tight lid, bring to a boil:
4 cups of water
2 cups of old fashioned oatmeal
1 teaspoon of salt

Use the old fashioned type of oats—big, hearty looking flakes. Instant oatmeal just doesn't cut it, nor do quick oats.

Lower heat to medium and simmer for as long as possible, adding a touch of boiling water when the mix gets too thick. Stir often.

Meanwhile—and I so hate meanwhile recipes, but sometimes there's no choice—toast a cup of unblanched almonds in the microwave for about five minutes, and when they start to smell lovely, take them out and chop them.

Add a couple tablespoons of preserves, apricot, raspberry or peach—to the oats along with the nuts. Serve with cream, brown sugar, and more of the preserves.

Blue Collar B & B

OVEN APPLE OATS

Preheat oven to 375°F.

In a saucepan, heat up 3½ cups of soy milk or ordinary milk until almost boiling.

Add:
1 cup of steel cut (often called Irish) *oats*
With 2 teaspoons maple syrup
½ teaspoon nutmeg
and about 1 cup of peeled and diced apples

Cook for a couple minutes, just until it all comes to a boil. Take it off the stove and stir in:

1 teaspoon salt and 2/3 cup raisins or currants

Put the whole mess into a good sized casserole—it has a tendency to boil over in the oven and stink up the house. Bake, stirring now and then, for about half an hour, or until your guests get up. Stir well before serving with milk or cream.

Bear with me; we're getting to the end of the mush section. You'll be amazed how many people request some version of it, and if you have diabetic guests, it's pretty much necessary. Use sugar-free preserves in that instance.

This next one sounds too healthy to taste good, and at first I had doubts about it. But, hey, try it. You and your guests will love it, trust me on this.

SLOW COOKER GRAIN AND SEED MUSH
(Quantity mix to keep on hand)

Mix together:
1 cup oat groats
½ cup barley groats
½ cup rye berries
½ cup whole almonds
¼ cup sunflower seeds
¼ cup pumpkin seeds

Store sealed until ready to use

When some brave, adventurous soul has ordered this:
Put 1 cup of the mix into a slow cooker before you go to bed
Add 4 cups water and a pinch of salt

Turn it to low, and hope the electricity doesn't go off before morning. Serve with the usual.

Now, upwards and onwards, remembering that every day we're getting better, better and better. Or at least our breakfasts are. Learn to make a really good French omelette. It's the simplest of all to concoct.

Blue Collar B & B

FRENCH OMELETTE, BLUE COLLAR STYLE

Heat a ten inch skillet on moderate, add a chunk of butter (don't let it brown).

In a small bowl, take a fork to three eggs, just breaking them up nicely.

Tip the eggs into the butter, and gently tip the pan and lift the edges of the eggs with a spatula to allow the uncooked stuff to get cooked—but gently.

When it still looks quite wet, sprinkle on salt, pepper, and basil— preferably chopped fresh leaves, but in my case probably dried.

With that trusty spatula, roll the thing into a sausage shape, slip on to a plate and decorate with whatever you have on hand— small tomatoes, cooked potatoes, bacon. The trick is not to overcook the eggs or muck it up with cheese and stuff.

That's it, pure and simple. Very French.

Now, moving on to pancakes, French toast and waffles. I don't use mixes because if guests do get around to making pancakes or waffles at home, chances are that's what they'll use. And we want to spoil them with the real thing, right? So here are a couple of great options, from a fantastic cookbook by my friend, Jeff Deraugh. His book is Firehall Cooking with Jeff The Chef. (My copy is stained, and the pages are coming loose, and I've written little notations like "fantastic" or "makes enough to feed a firehall.")

Bobby Hutchinson

BUTTERMILK GRIDDLE CAKES

Heat a griddle, not smoking hot, but moderate, to about 300°F to 350°F.

In a big bowl cream:
4 eggs
¼ cup white sugar
2 tablespoons vegetable oil

In a smaller bowl combine:
1 cup unbleached flour
1 cup whole wheat flour
1 teaspoon salt
1 teaspoon baking powder
1 teaspoon baking soda

Add dry to creamed, along with 2 cups buttermilk

Let it sit while you have a cup of tea. (Pancake batters seem to need to rest a lot; I have no idea why when the cook is the one who's usually exhausted.) You can add a fistful of blueberries if you're big on antioxidents. Then bake them on that moderately hot griddle, using small spoonfuls. When they bubble, flip them over—but only once, so be sure they're golden brown before you do. You can do all this a little while before your guests make their entrance if you tent the cooked ones with foil and tuck them into a warm oven.

BLUE COLLAR B & B

MY SWEET POTATO PANCAKES

Peel and grate enough yam or sweet potato to make 1 cup. Dump into a big measuring cup

Add:
A little grated lemon peel
2 eggs
1 cup of milk
2 tablespoons melted butter

In a bowl:
Sift 1 cup unbleached flour
2 teaspoons baking powder
½ teaspoon salt
2 tablespoons sugar

Gently stir dry into wet and let it all rest about ten minutes. Heat a griddle to moderate, use small tablespoonfuls, and cook until golden.

JEFF'S BEST BUTTERMILK WAFFLES

With a whisk:
*Blend 1 cup whole wheat flour
With 1 cup unbleached white*

Add:
*1 teaspoon baking soda
½ teaspoon salt
½ teaspoon cinnamon
2 tablespoons brown sugar*

In two other bowls:
*Separate 2 eggs and to the yolks
Add 1/3 cup melted butter
2 cups buttermilk*

Whip the whites with an electric mixer until they're stiff. Fold into yolk mixture. In a preheated waffle iron, put about 1/3 cup of batter, close the lid and let it sit for about 4 minutes. You can do this a little ahead of time, but not a lot. Waffles dry out.

There will come those blessed times when there's no room left at the Inn, and while you're mentally adding up how much of your line of credit you can pay off thanks to a full house, you're also making breakfast for eight or more people. That's when you don't hand out menus. You just get up extra early, make generous amounts of scones and muffins, add a pot of oatmeal and double the recipe for pancakes, and rely on one or two of the following good stick-to-the-ribs farmer's fare, notable because they can be made the night before.

FRENCH TOAST

Before you go to bed, mix:
1 dozen eggs
½ cup cream
½ teaspoon vanilla
grated zest of 1 orange
2 tablespoons of orange liqueur in a 9 by 13 inch pan

Place slices of 1 loaf French bread over mixture, making sure slices are well coated. Cover with plastic wrap, place in fridge overnight. Next morning, take bread slices out and lay on well-greased cookie sheet. Bake at 375°F for 25 minutes. Serve with fruit or maple syrup.

BOBBY HUTCHINSON

OVERNIGHT CINNAMON BUNS

Again before bed, grease a 10 inch Bundt pan.

Add 20 frozen dough rolls
(Supermarket bakeries will have these on hand, ask for them)

Sprinkle the rolls with:
1 cup brown sugar
¼ cup vanilla instant pudding
1 tablespoon cinnamon
¾ cup of raisins
½ cup melted butter

Cover with a clean damp cloth, leaving out at room temperature. In the morning, preheat the oven to 350°F, put a cookie sheet under the Bundt pan (it often runs over) and bake for 25 minutes. Let sit for 5 minutes and turn out on a pretty plate.

Blue Collar B & B

MORNING HOST SANITY SAVER
(You need 16 slices of white bread for this)

Put 8 pieces of bread in a 9 by 13 inch buttered glass baking dish. Cover dish entirely, including sides. Cover bread with slices of back bacon or ham and slices of sharp cheddar.

> In a bowl:
> Beat 6 eggs
> ½ teaspoon pepper
> 1 teaspoon dry mustard
> ¼ cup minced onion
> ¼ cup chopped green pepper
> 2 teaspoons Worcestershire sauce
> 3 cups whole milk and a dash of Tabasco.

Pour this mess over the bread thing, cover it and stick it in the fridge overnight. In the morning, melt ¼ pound butter and pour over top, then sprinkle with enough Special K or cornflakes to cover. Bake at 350°F, uncovered. Let sit 10 minutes and then serve.

Now, last but not least, a really good egg casserole. You do this one in the morning, but it saves you from the insanity of trying to keep an eye on two eggs poaching, four eggs frying, six eggs boiling—and the damned bacon which is shrivelling up to nothing as you watch, to say nothing of the pancakes, which are burning.

(A good solution for bacon is to buy only thick slices, dip them in flour, put them in a cold frying pan over moderate heat and then before they finish cooking, put in your oven, still warm from those scones and muffins you made earlier. Let the bacon go on cooking until its time to eat.)

Or you can specify that you only host vegetarians.

Bobby Hutchinson

A REALLY GOOD EGG CASSEROLE
(You need to thaw out 2 cups of shredded hash brown potatoes for this one)

Butter a two quart casserole dish
Preheat the oven to 350°F

Beat a dozen eggs with 1 cup of plain yogurt
(A word of caution here: I made my own yogurt and it was a little runny. The centre of the casserole didn't gel, so now I use only bought yogurt.)

Melt 1/3 cup of butter gently, lightly sautéing ¼ cup of chopped onion with a teaspoon of MSG-free seasoning salt. (There's a good one called Johnny's.)

Add:
2 cups of thawed hash browns

Stir to mix, pour in egg mixture and stir a little to blend. Pour into casserole dish, top with 1 cup grated cheddar. Bake for 25 minutes or more, until a knife comes out clean.

There are many other delicious things out there to feed guests in the morning, and the eager host will experiment with lots of different recipes, always remembering that the most important ingredient is love. Love poured lavishly into the flour and sugar always makes everything taste better.

Finally, there's a motto I kept as a reminder, just inside the door of the armoire where I stored guests' coats, and where I noticed it daily. It seemed the best advice I'd ever come by for running a B&B. It's by Mother Teresa, and it says:

> LET NO ONE EVER COME TO YOU
>
> WITHOUT LEAVING BETTER AND HAPPIER.
>
> BE THE LIVING EXPRESSION OF GOD'S KINDNESS,
>
> KINDNESS IN YOUR FACE, KINDNESS IN YOUR EYES,
>
> KINDNESS IN YOUR SMILE.

I didn't always succeed—some guests at the Blue Collar were more challenging than others, and my final encounter with Louie was my most regrettable mistake—but I usually tried my very best. And maybe that's all we can do.

Thanks for listening.
May your B&B bring you the joy
and laughter mine brought me.

******

ABOUT THE AUTHOR

Bobby Hutchinson runs the Blue Collar B&B in Sparwood, B.C., Canada. In her spare time she writes books, shamelessly harvesting stories from agreeable guests. She has more than forty-five published books and is working on a dozen more. Apart from guests, she lives alone, walks, works out at Curves, meditates, reads and cooks. Her current challenge is applying the concept, When you change the way you look at a thing, the thing you look at changes.